DESERT

published in conjunction with the exhibition *Desert*
March 12 - April 23, 2011 at The Company, Los Angeles

introduction: Anat Ebgi

images and sequencing : Jesse Fleming

interview: Amanda Law

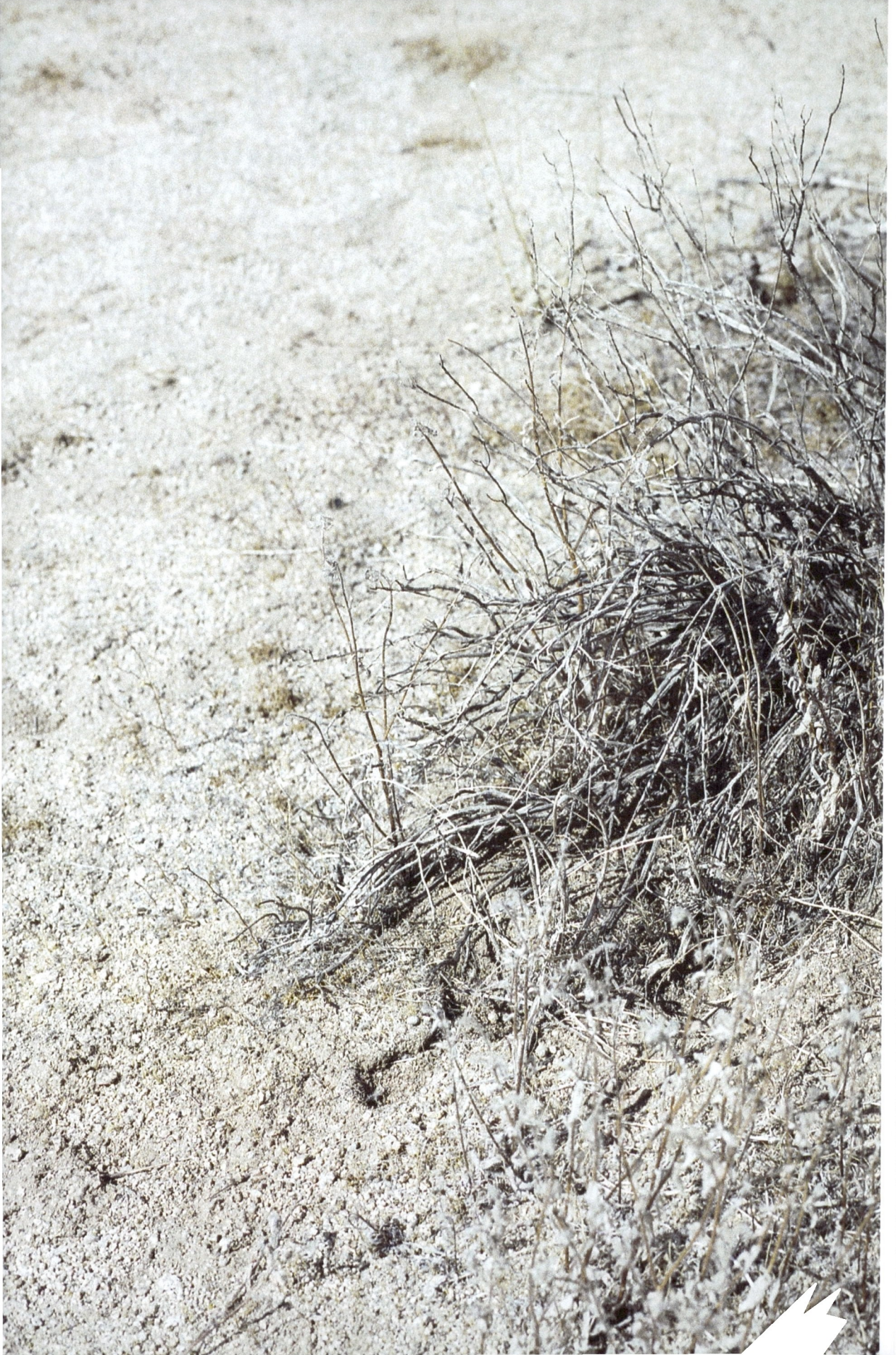

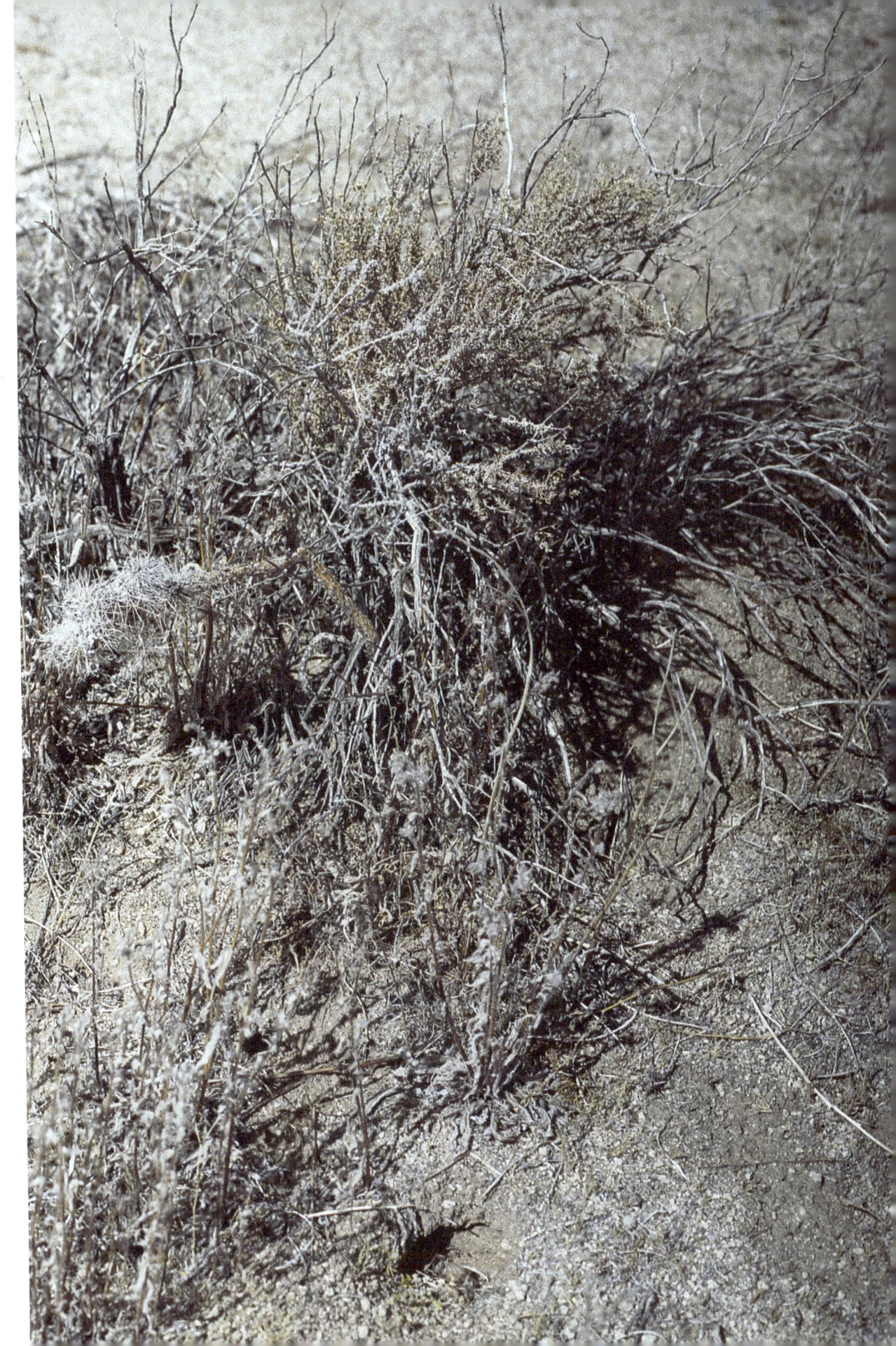

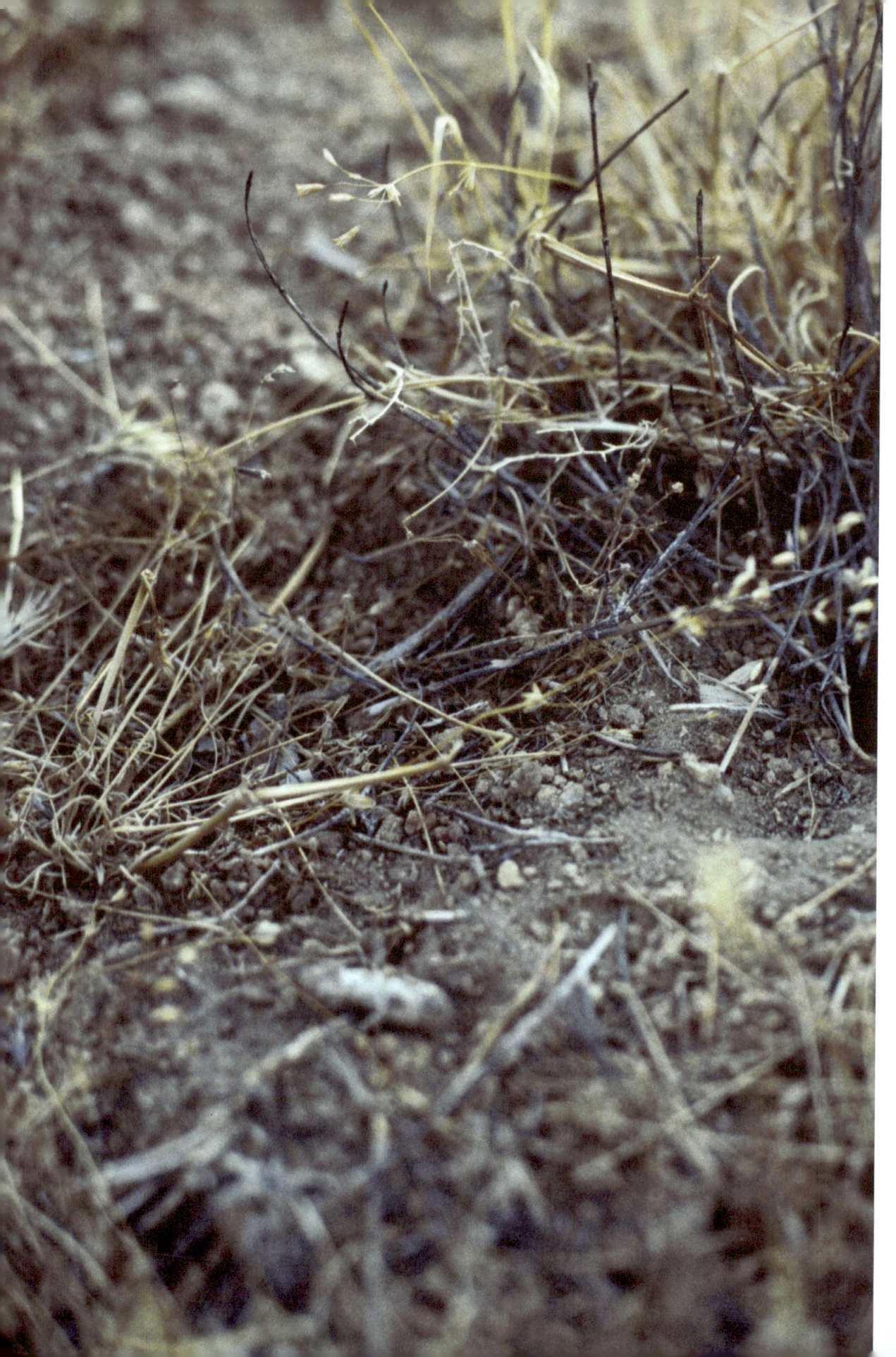

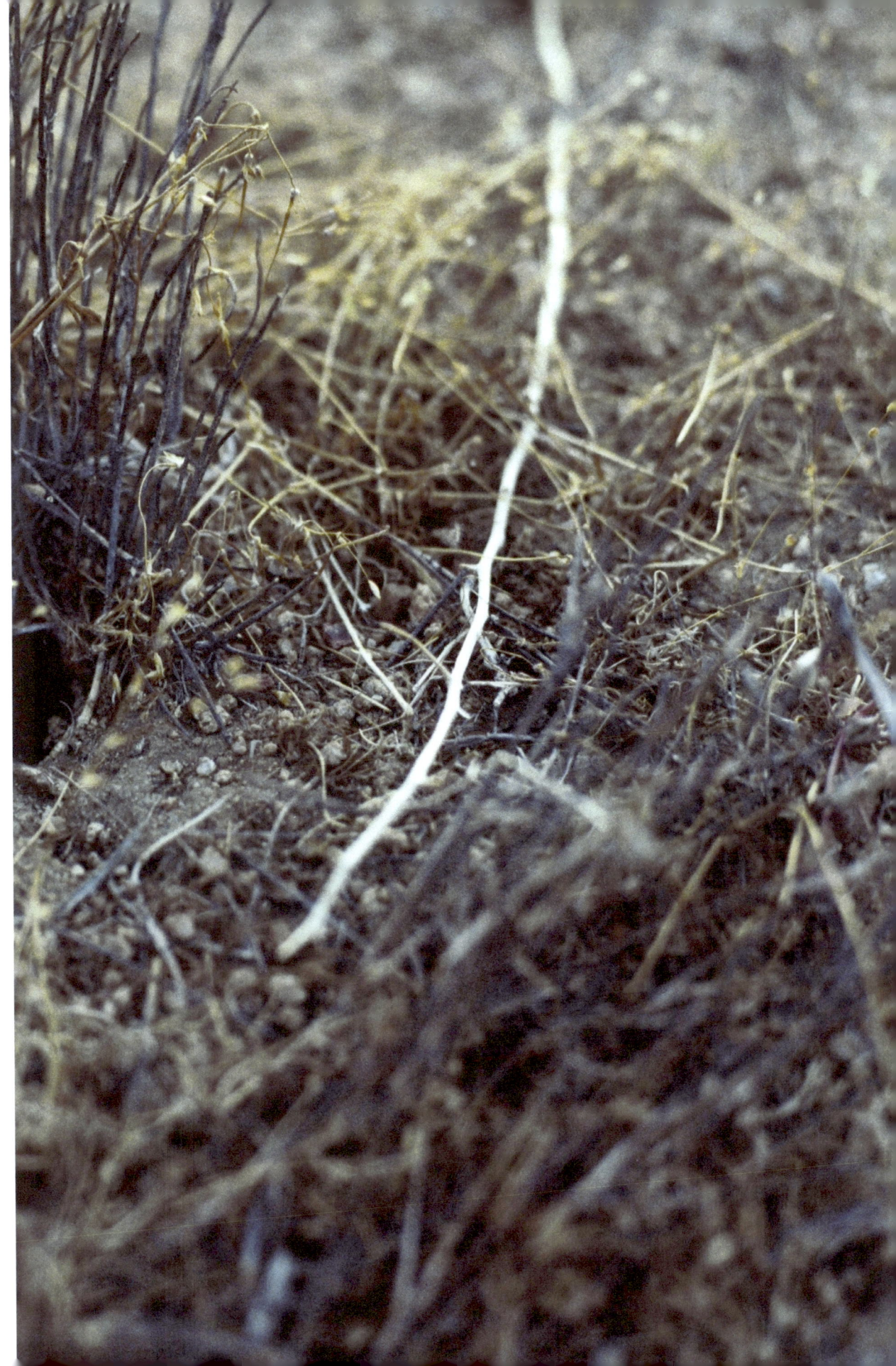

The Widening Circles of Jesse Fleming
For the occasion of the exhibition *Desert*, at The Company, March 12 – April 23, 2011
by Anat Ebgi

I live my life in widening circles
that reach out across the world.
I may not complete this last one
but I give myself to it.

I circle around God, around the primordial tower.
I've been circling for thousands of years
and I still don't know: am I a falcon,
a storm, or a great song?
-- Ranier Maria Rilke, from Rilke's Book of Hours: Love Poems to God

Jesse Fleming approaches his work as a disciplined observer. This is evident in three
of his recent videos: *Birds (Apart/Together)*, 2009, *Methods of Invisibility*, 2010, and
Desert, 2011. In all three works, Fleming sets out to document the intricacies that exist in daily
life, capturing them on video, editing, and finally associating the footage to sound.

In *Birds (Apart/Together)*, 2009, Fleming spent months filming homing pigeons from a Brooklyn
rooftop. The video is broken into three parts or perspectives: the macro structure of the birds, the
individuals composing the group, and the individual point of view. The mesmerizing flight
patterns of the flock mimic human flow of the city below; the cooing pigeons sublimate the
noises of the city. *Birds* is a hypnotic visual and auditory meditation on objectivity.

Two months prior to September 11th 2001, Fleming bought a retired police car in Southern
California, unmarked gray uniforms, and drove across the country to New York, documenting his
journey. The result of the footage was *Methods of Invisibility*, a highly edited, paranoid, video
game like experience that captures the stares and erratic behavior of the people on the freeways
and gas stations when confronted with authority. With a camera affixed to the dashboard,
Fleming played into fear and the surveillance state that the Bush years enforced.

With the newest work, *Desert*, Fleming observes life in the arid landscape. *Desert* (2010), was
shot in California's Joshua Tree National Park, 140 miles east of Los Angeles. The park is over
1200 square miles of high altitude desert with bizarre geological features. The edited footage
captures the sublime cycles within the desert landscape – the shifting position of the sun, clouds,
and the movement of the desert plants by the wind. The hypnotic pace of the desert is interrupted
by aerial shots of crop circle-like patterns in the flat valley. The patterns evoke Michael Heizer's
motorcycle markings, Circular Planar Displacement Drawing, where tire marks etched the sand
to be erased by first rain.

A selection of photographs from *Desert* will be exhibited along with photographs from the
ethereal *It* series. *It* distills the content of *Desert* to shape, sound, light, color, and atmospheric
perspective. The video *It* will also be shown along with sound component. Being influenced by
the work of Michael Snow and Robert Irwin as well as science of brain entrainment and
psychoacoustics, Fleming's work incorporates visuals and audio to construct an experiential
journey.

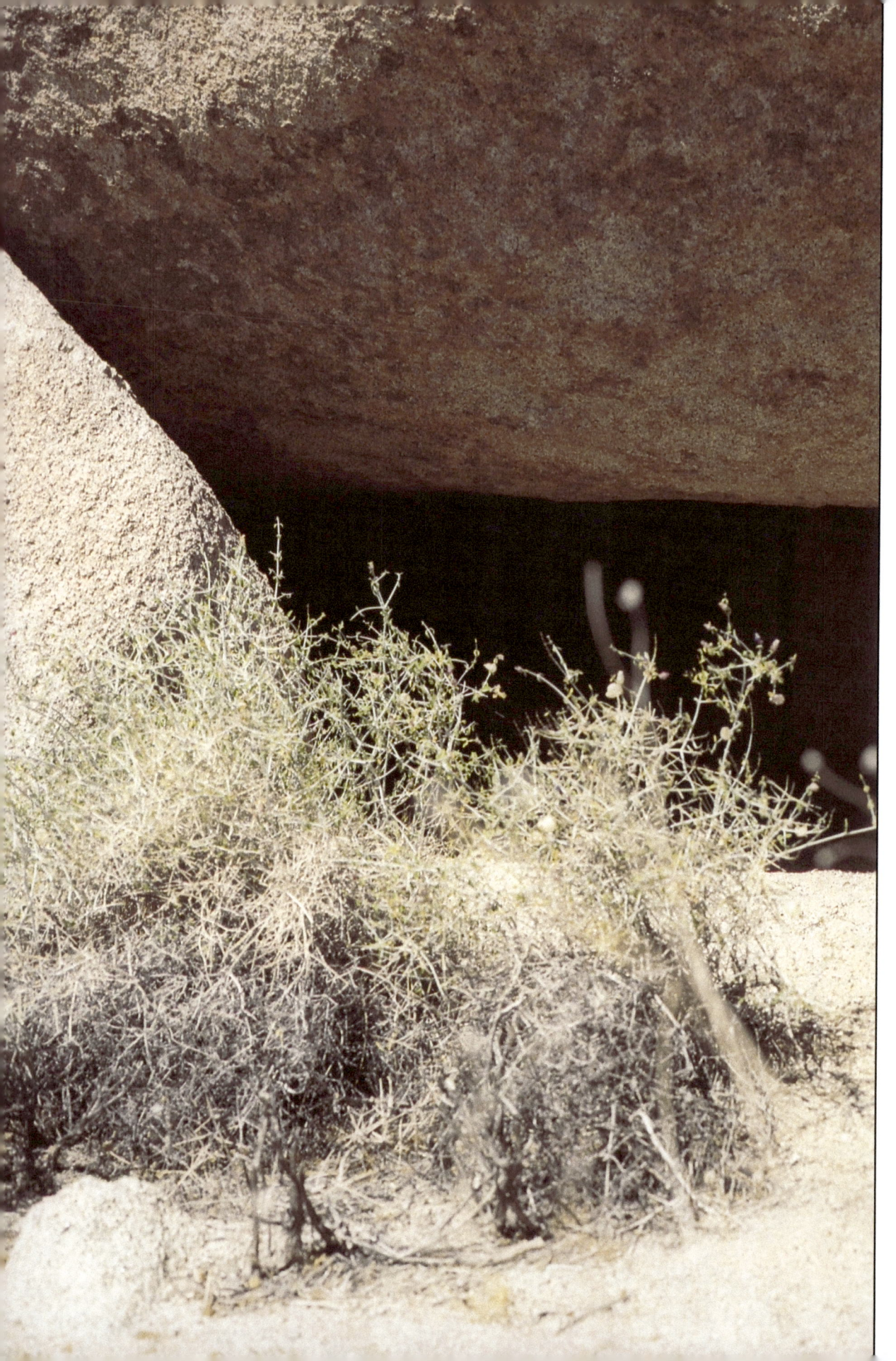

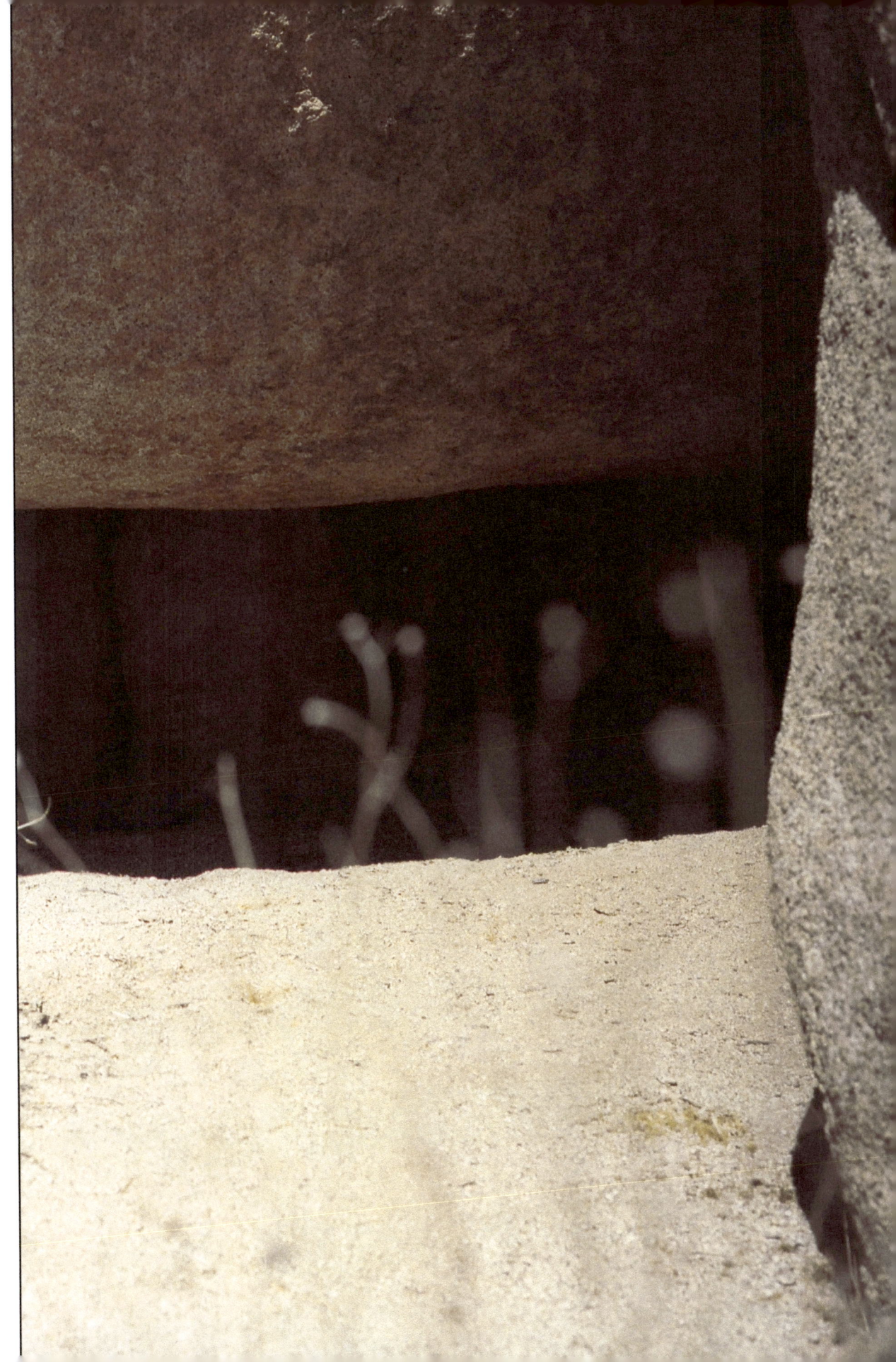

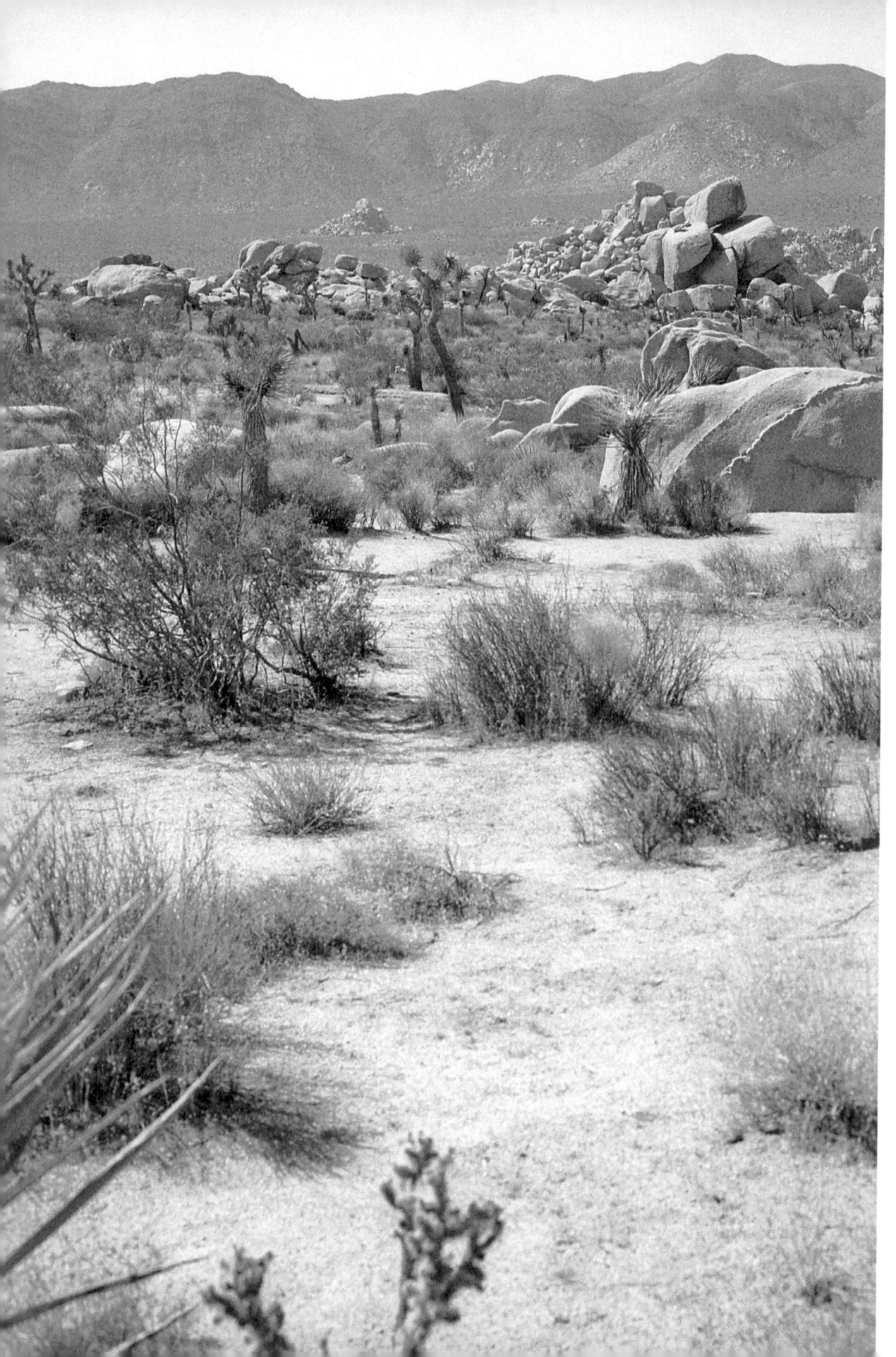

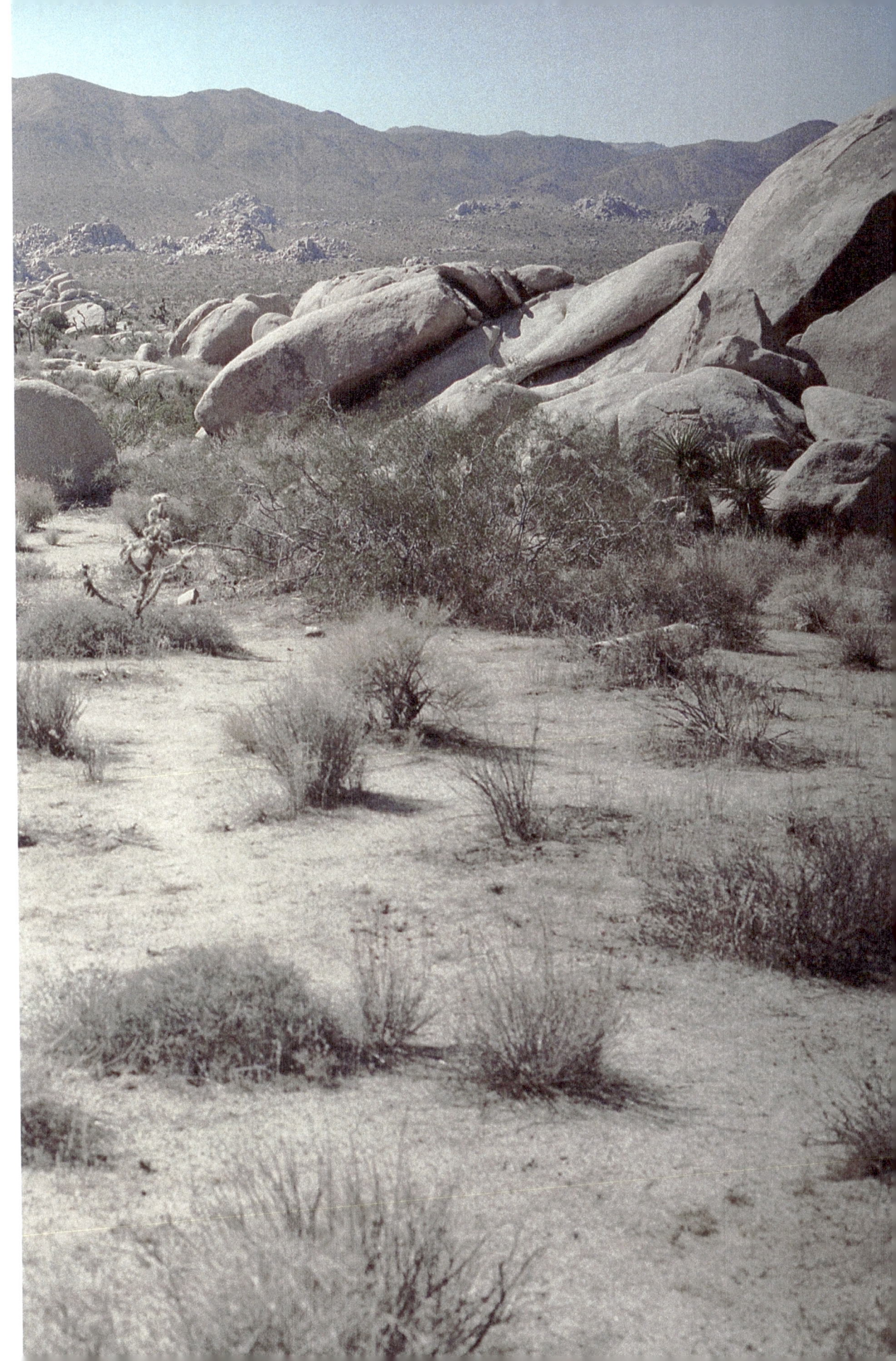

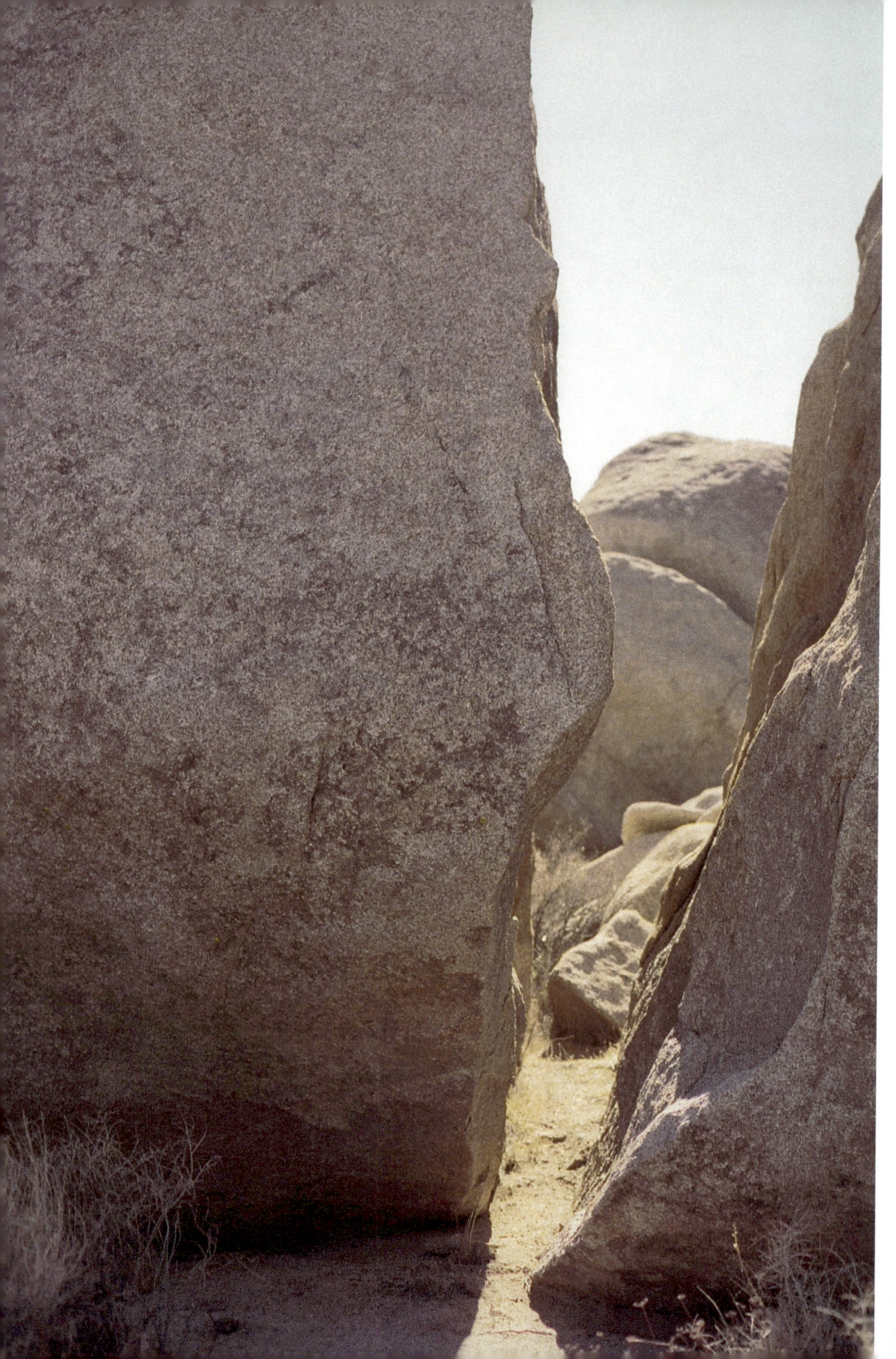

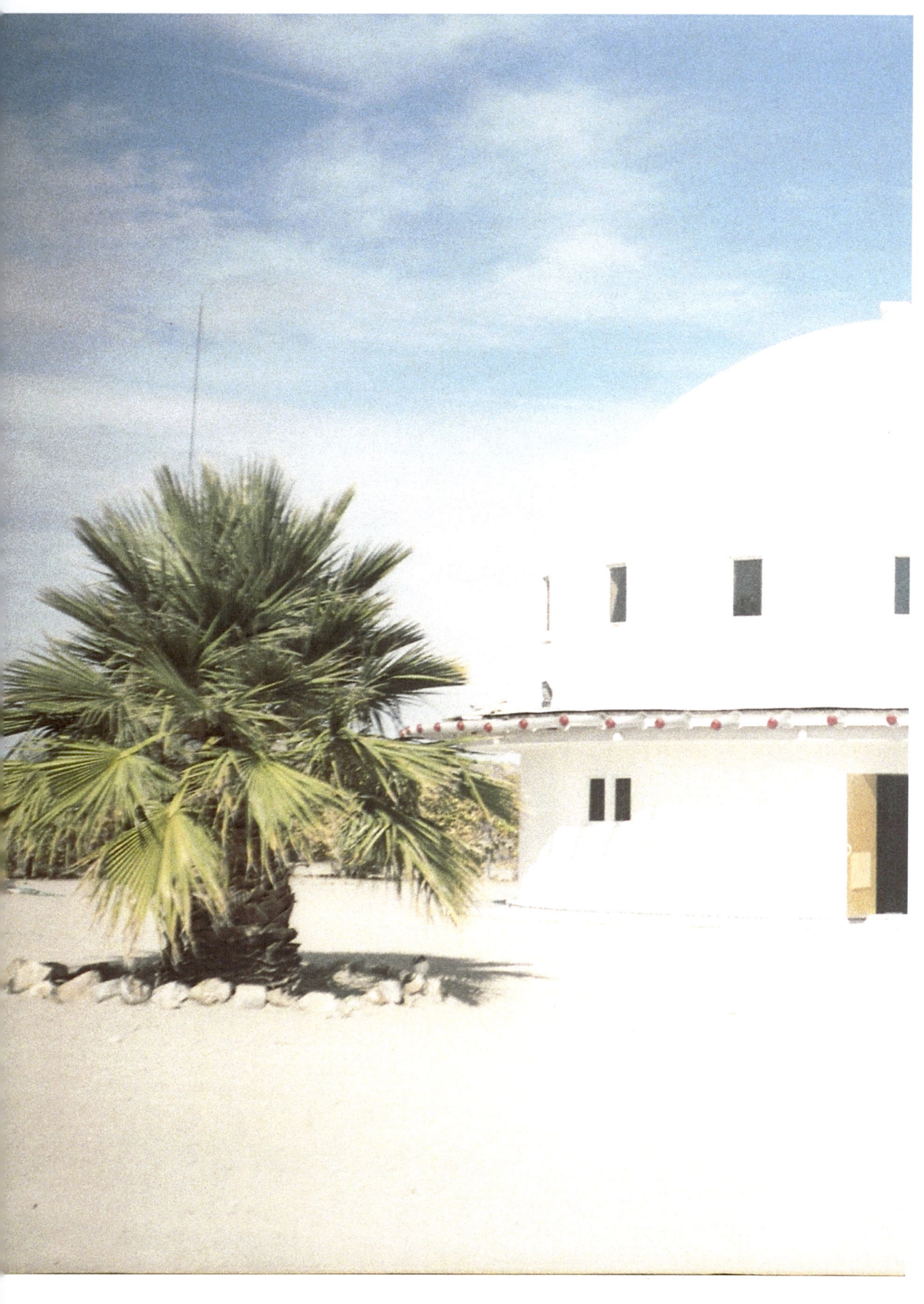

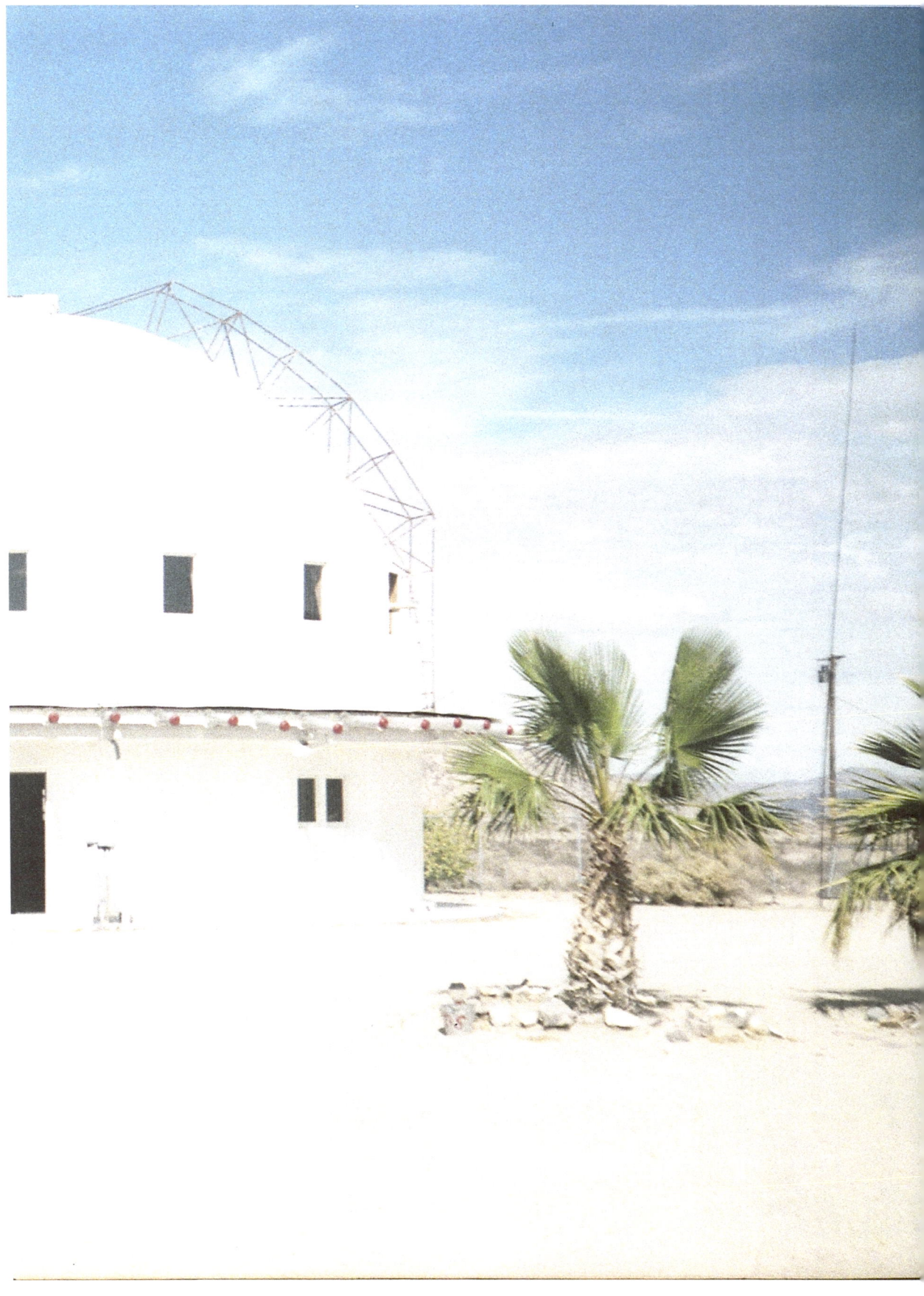

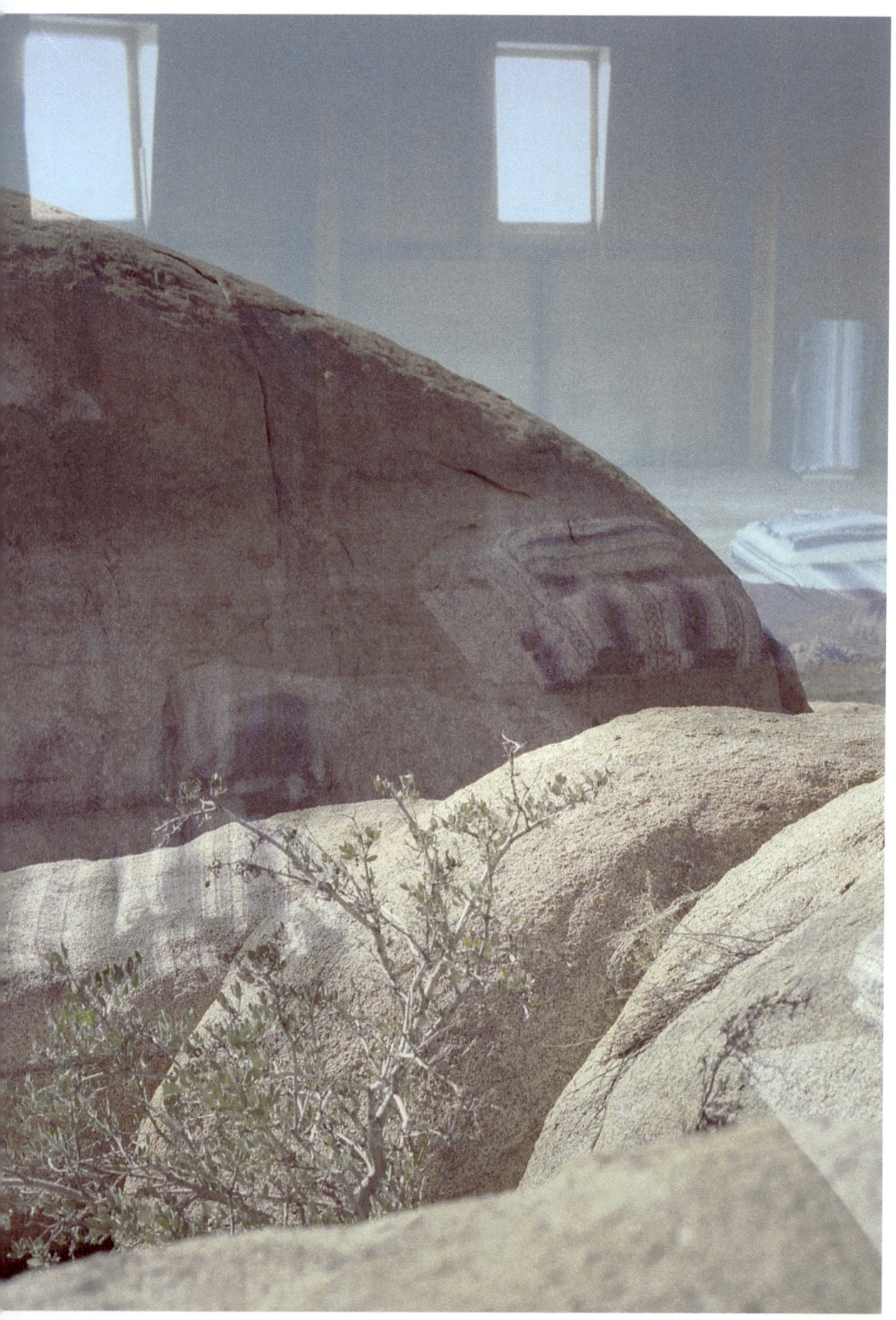

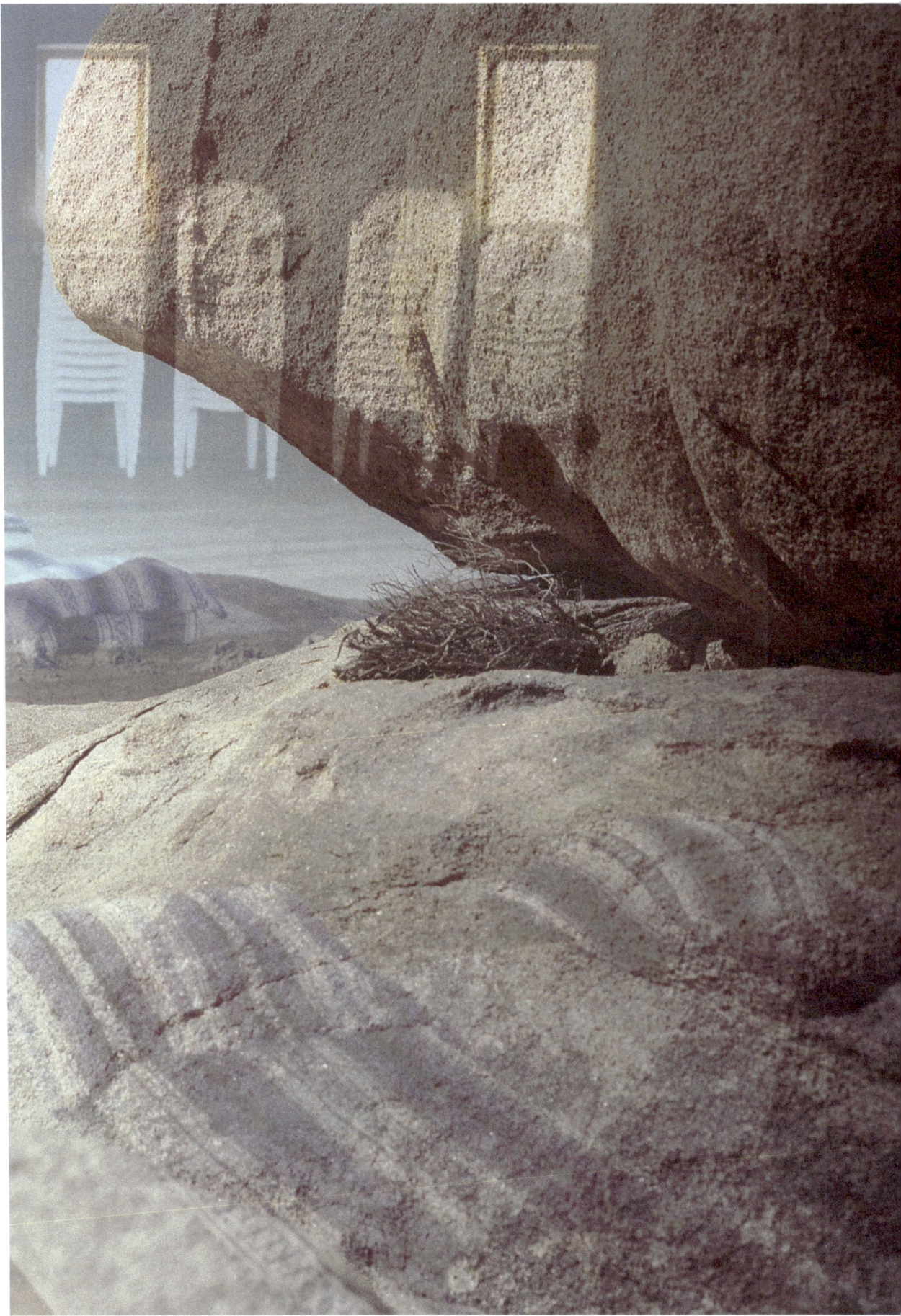

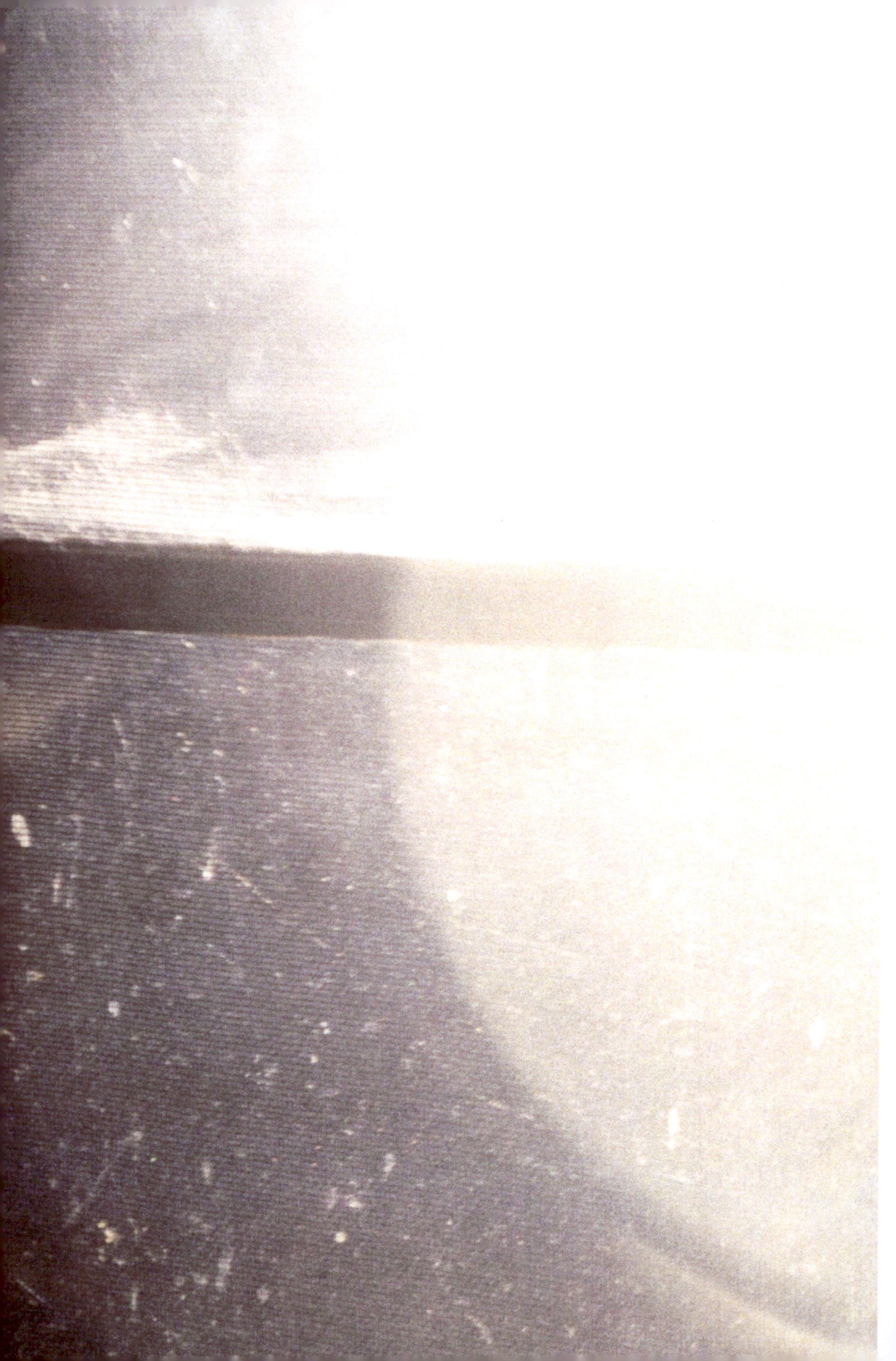

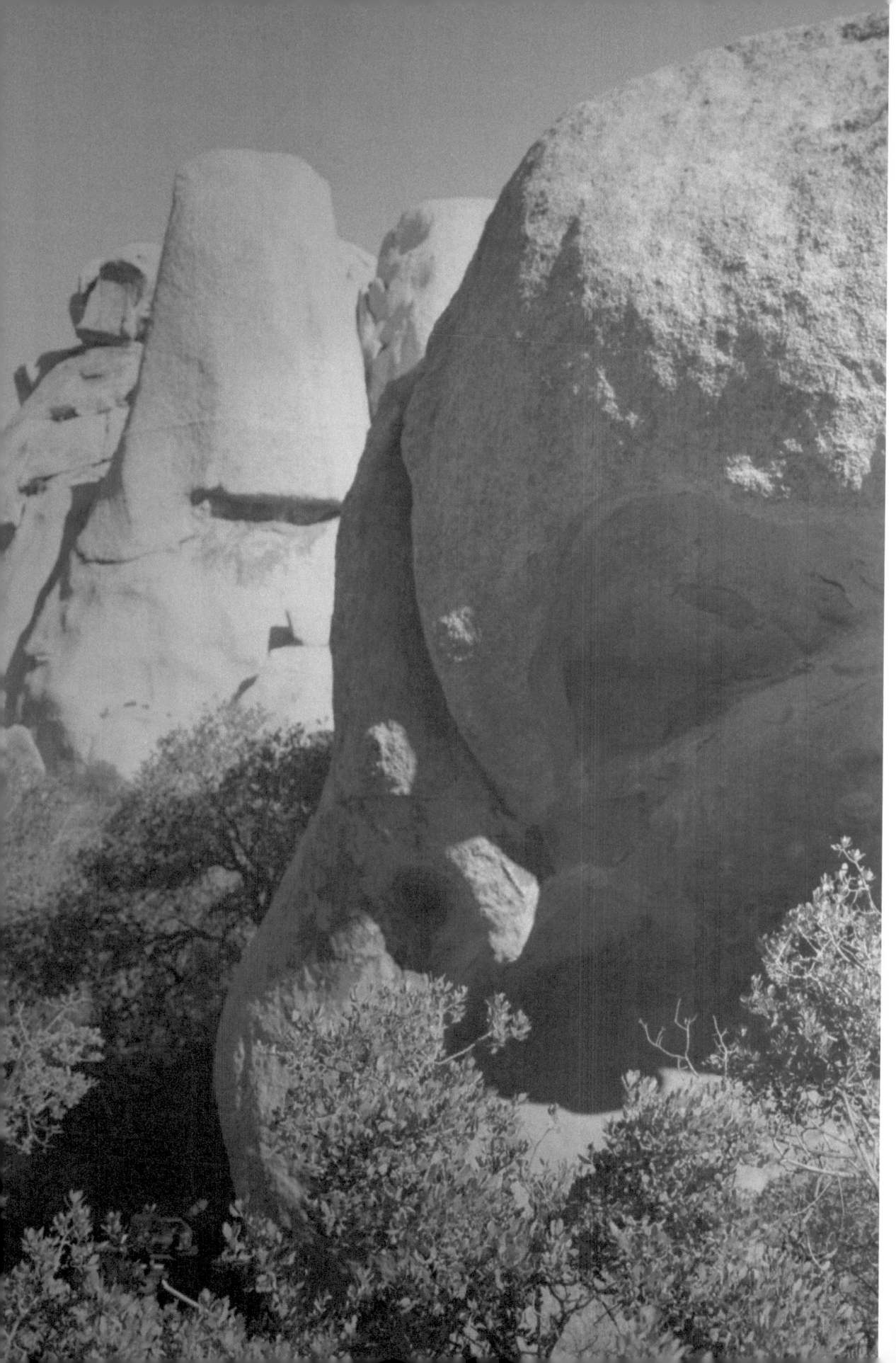

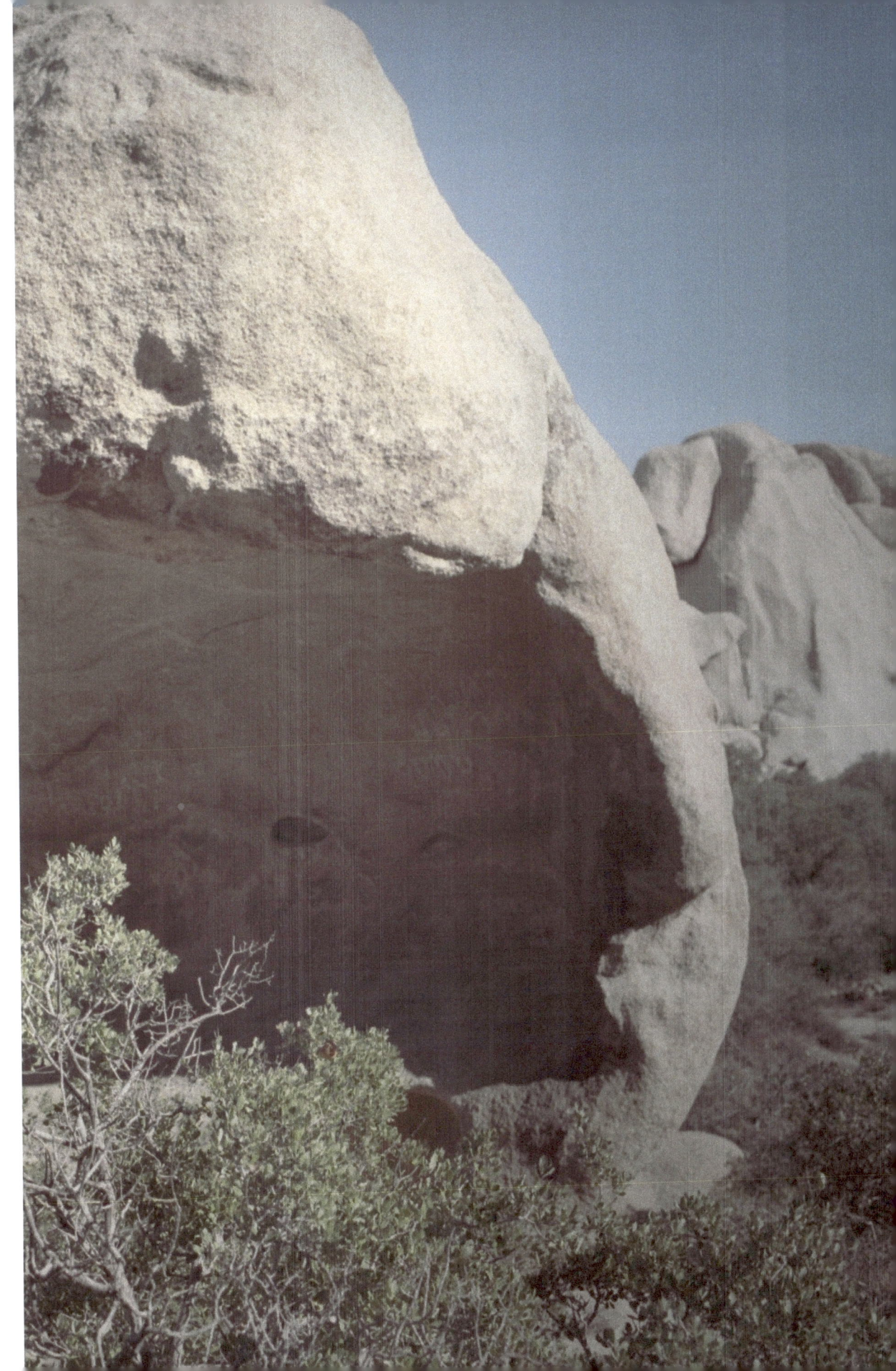

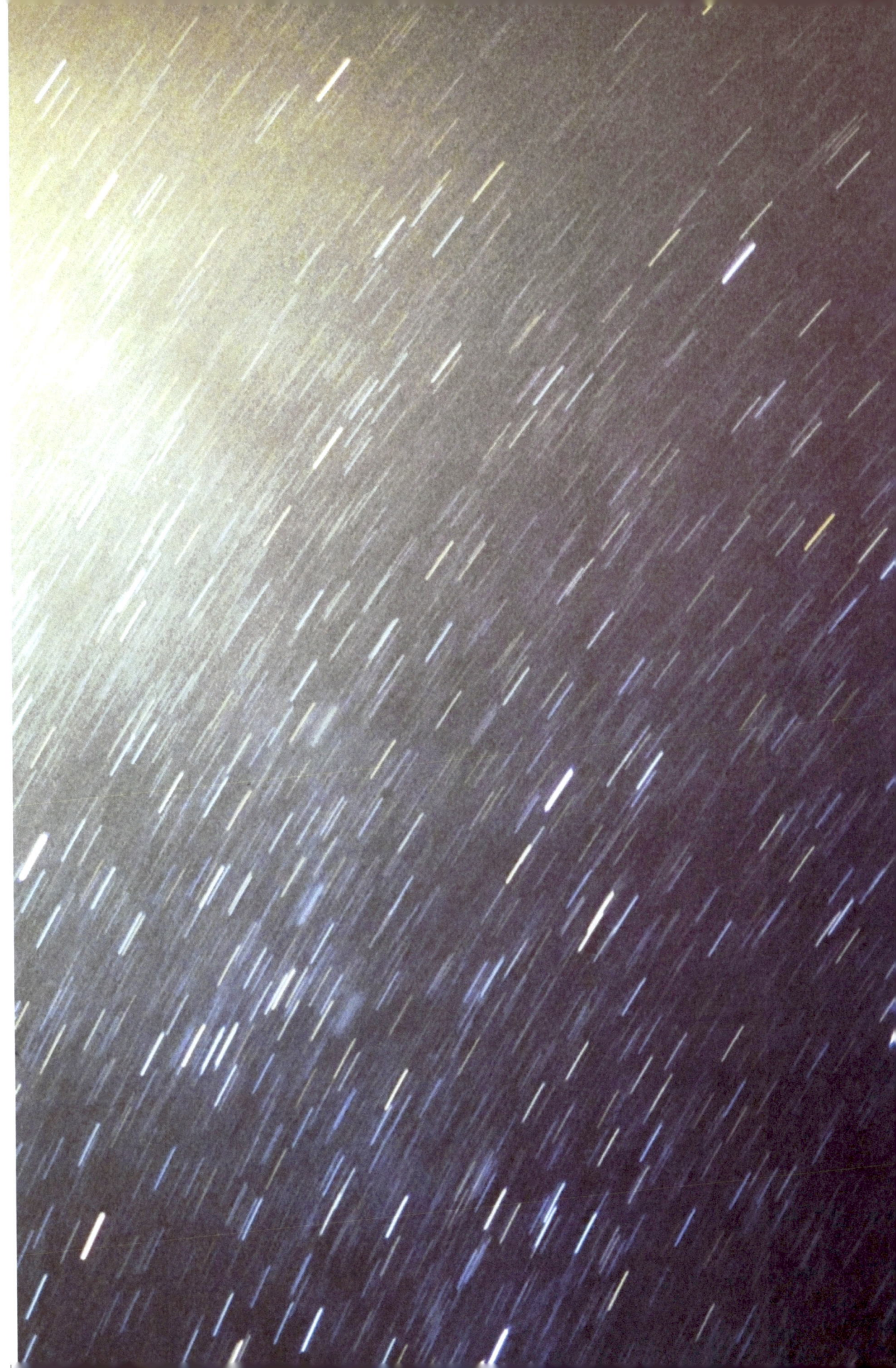

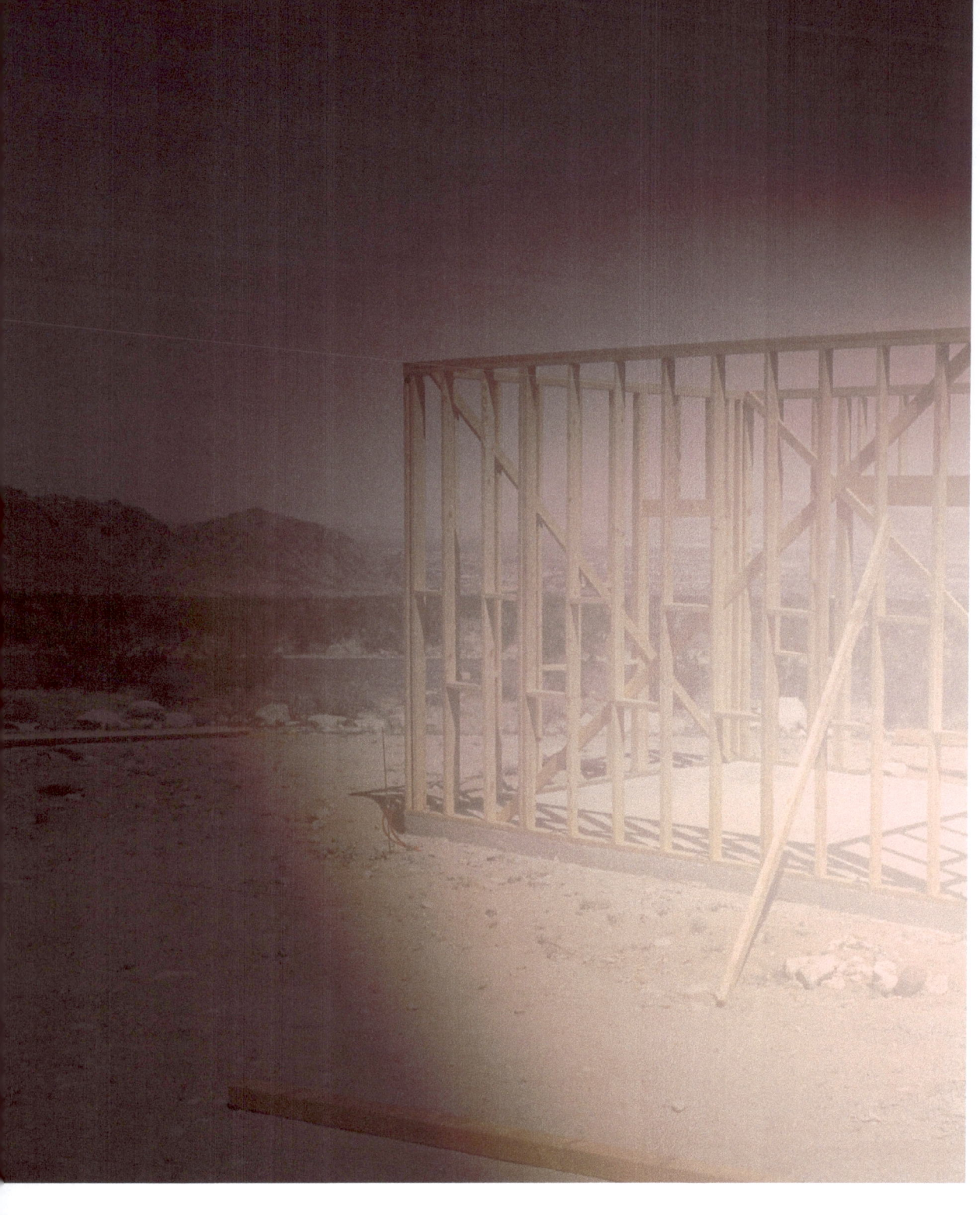

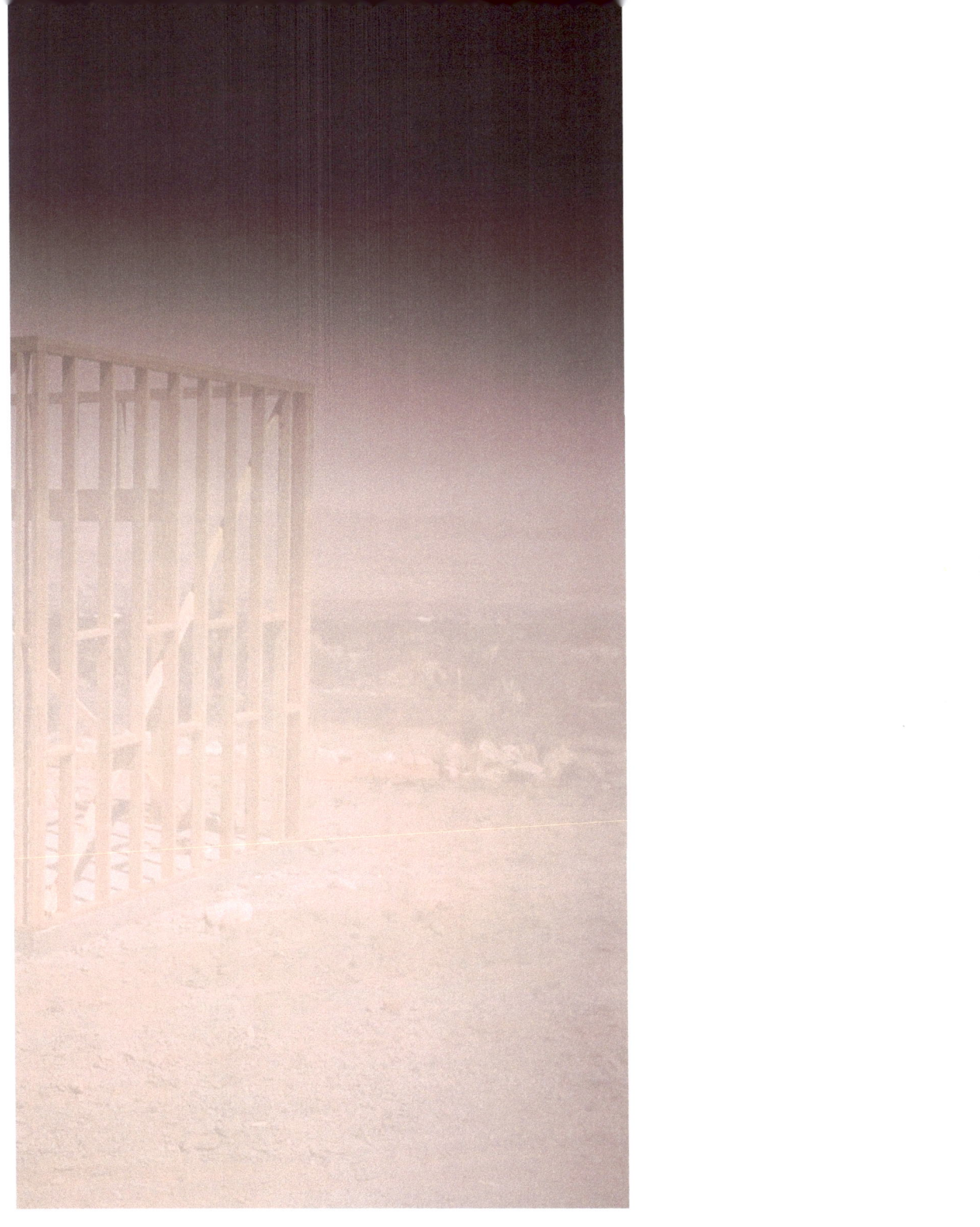

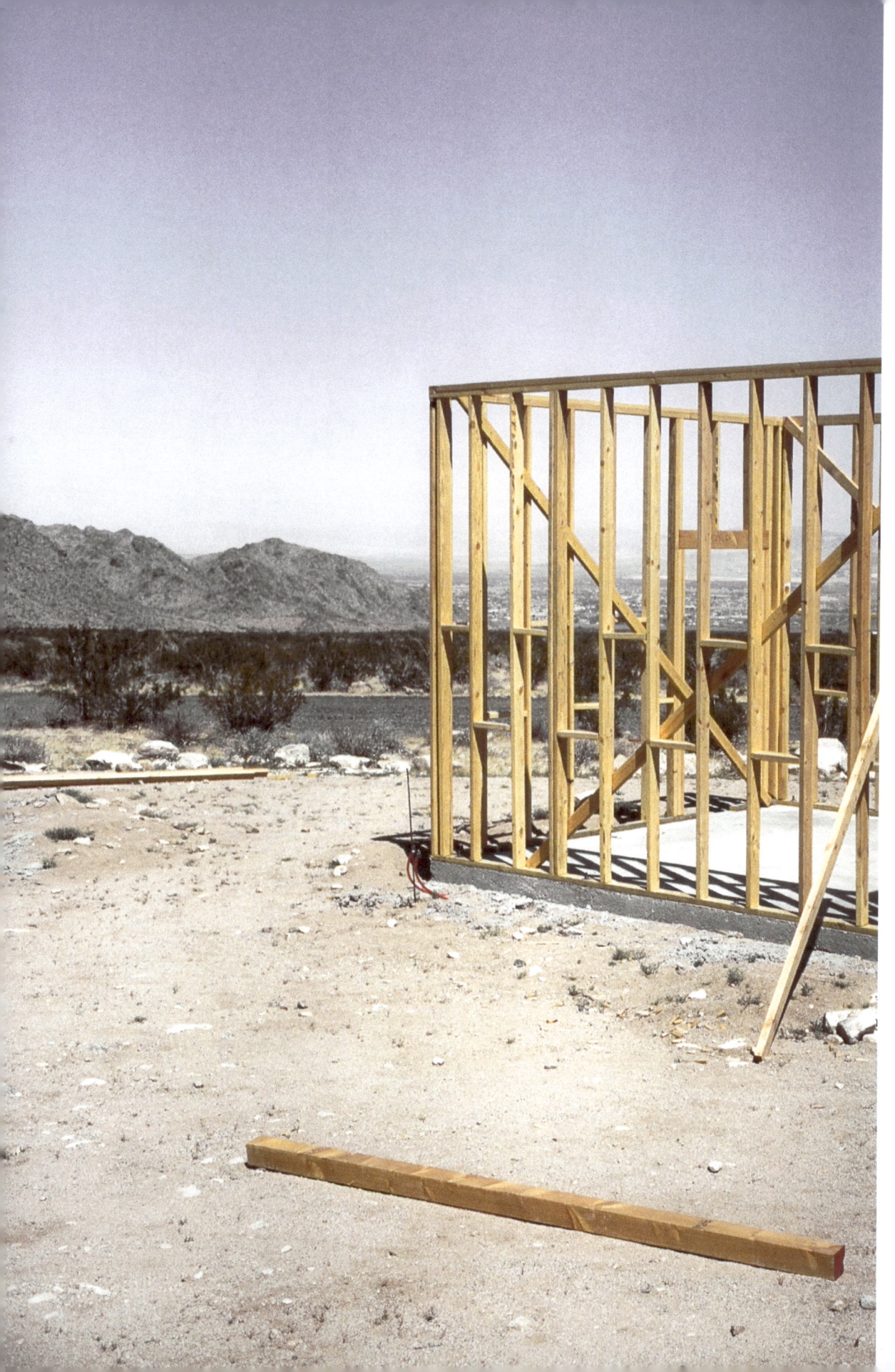

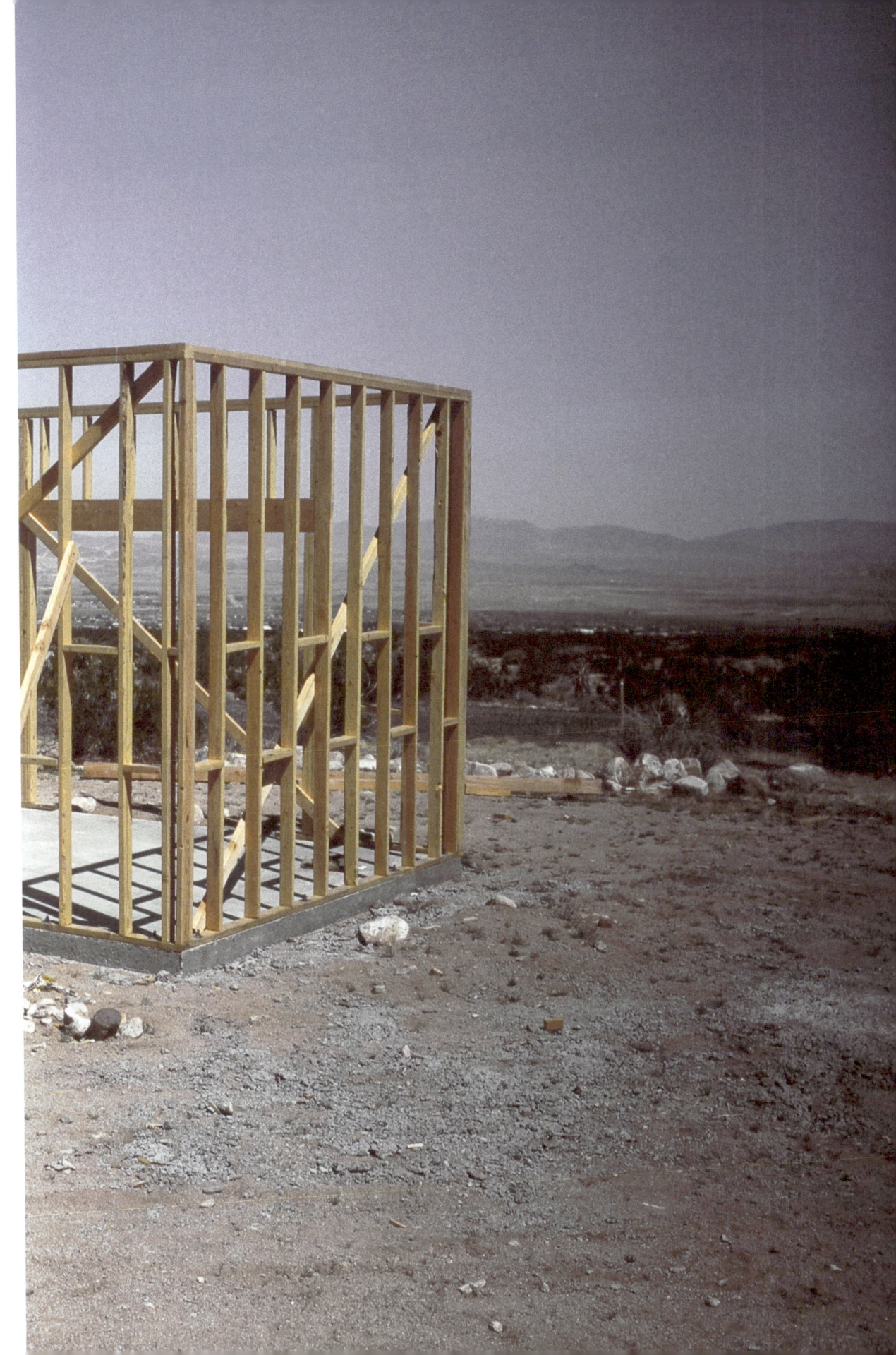

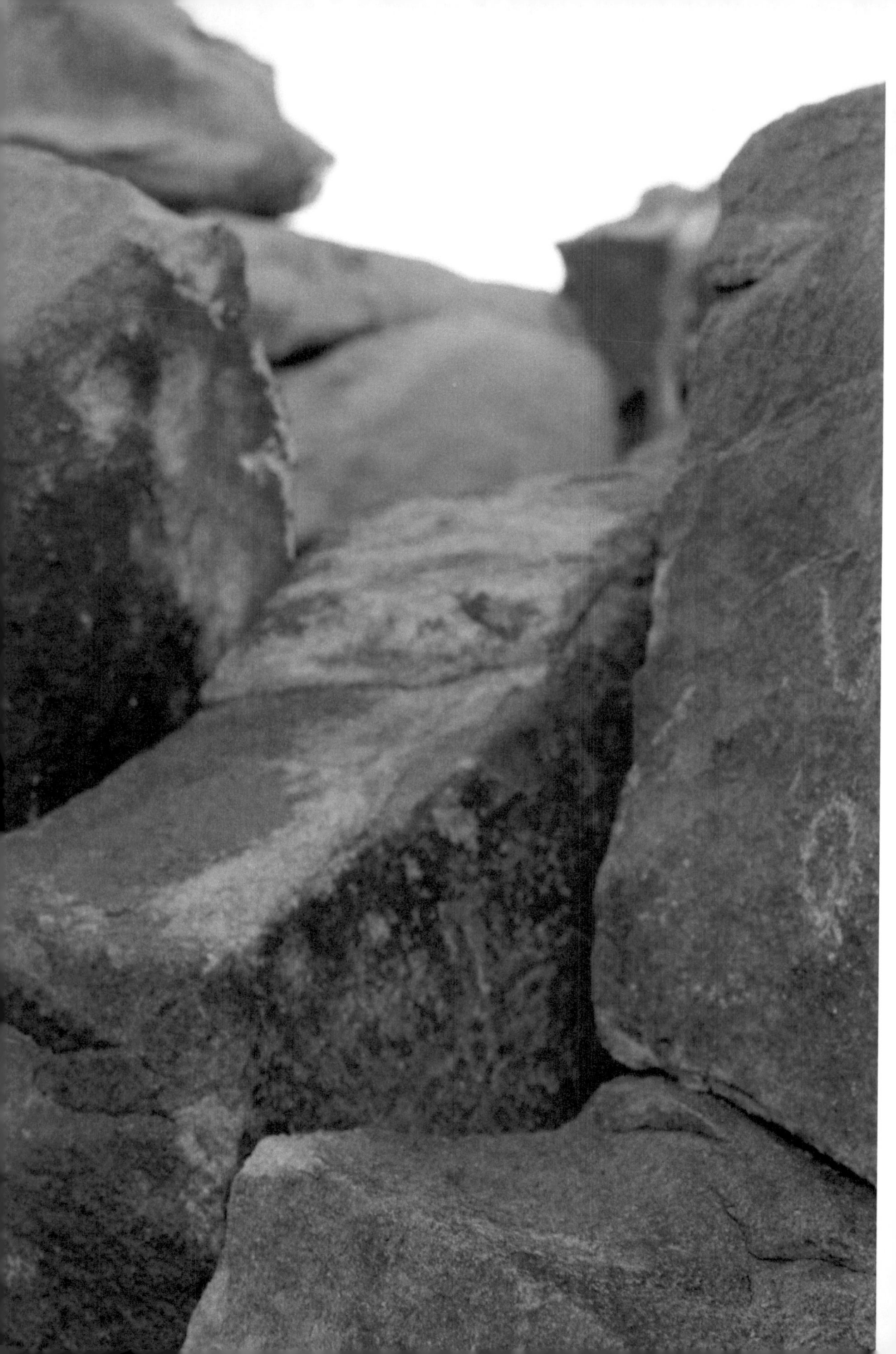

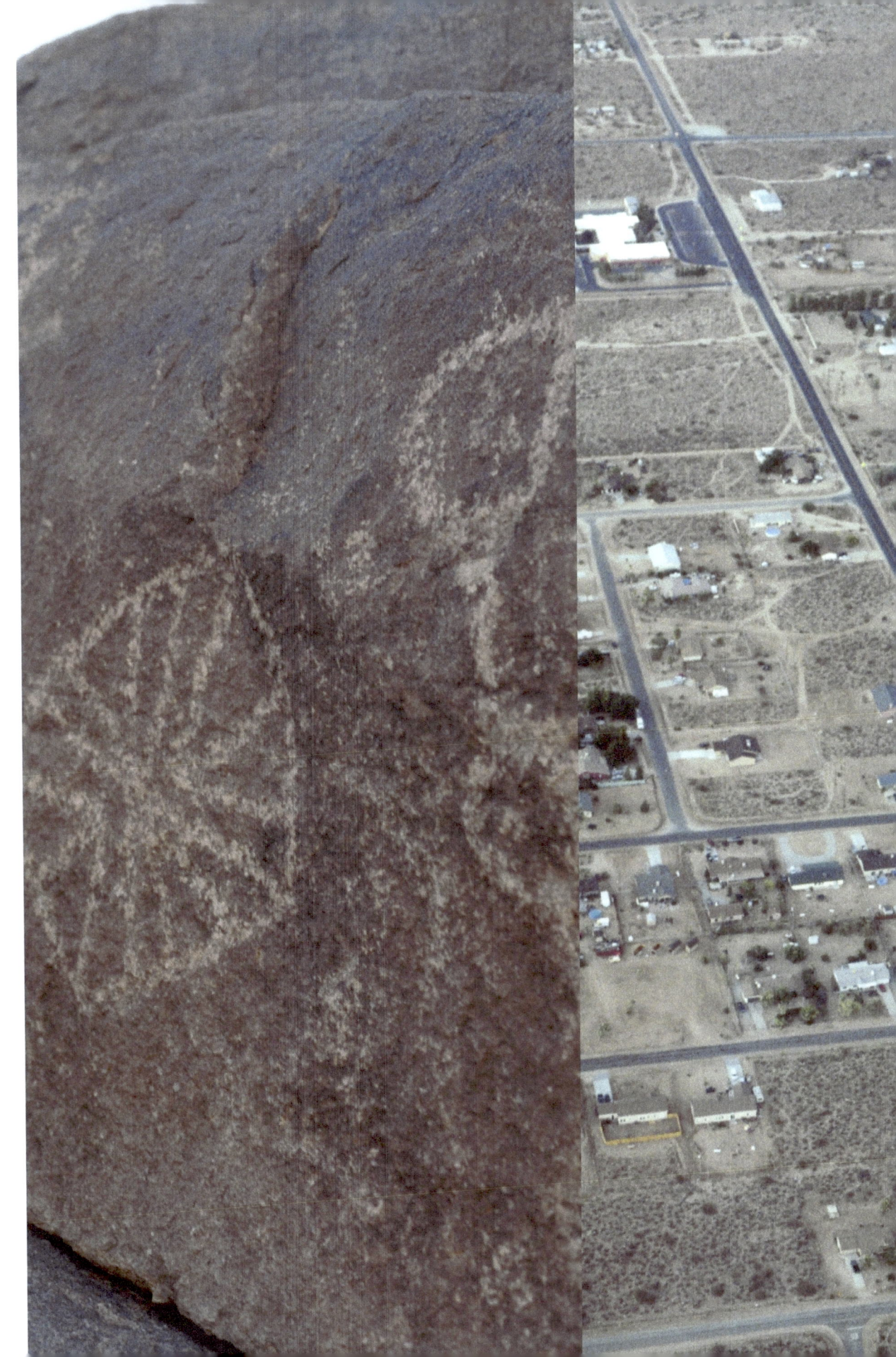

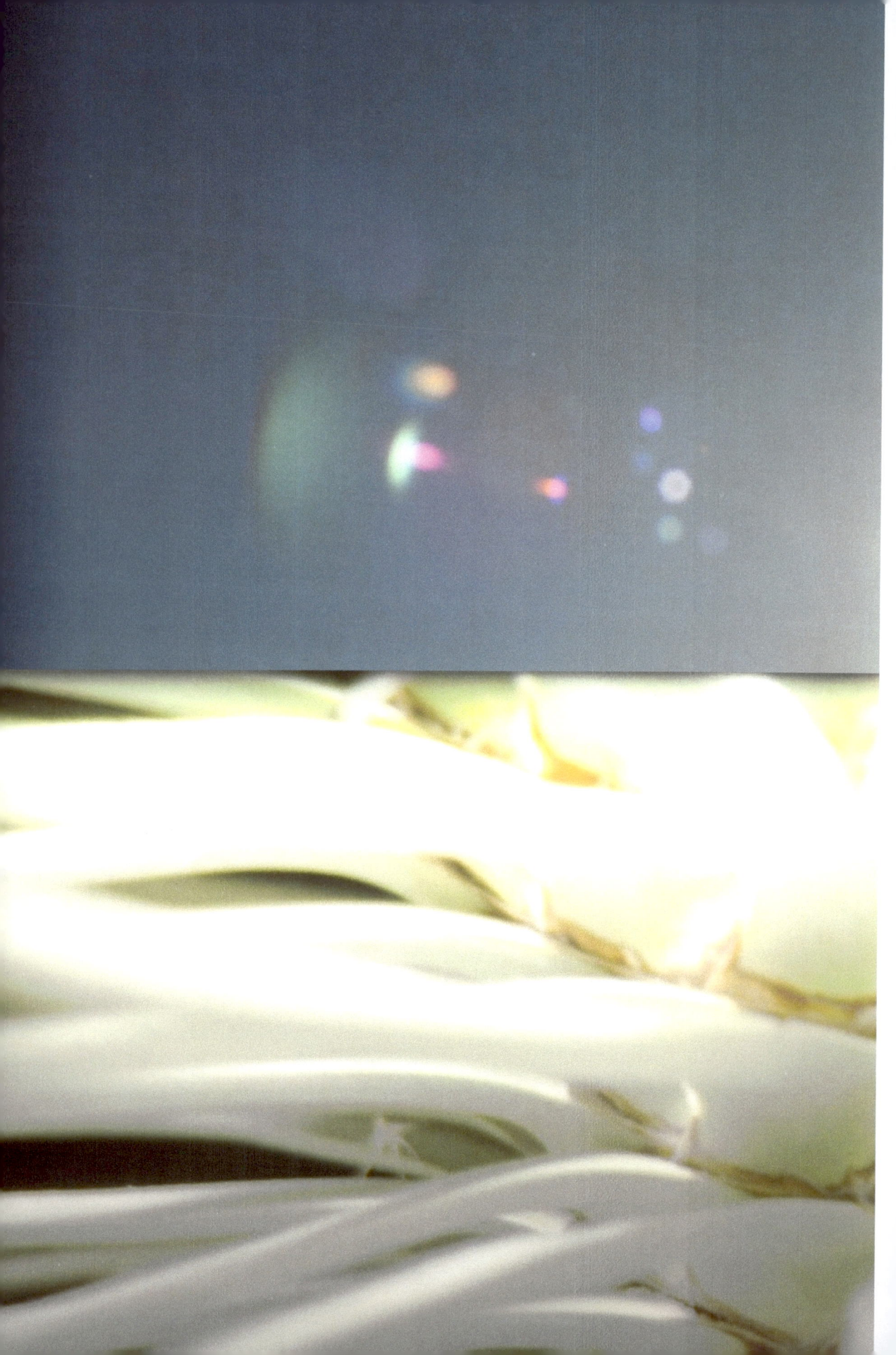

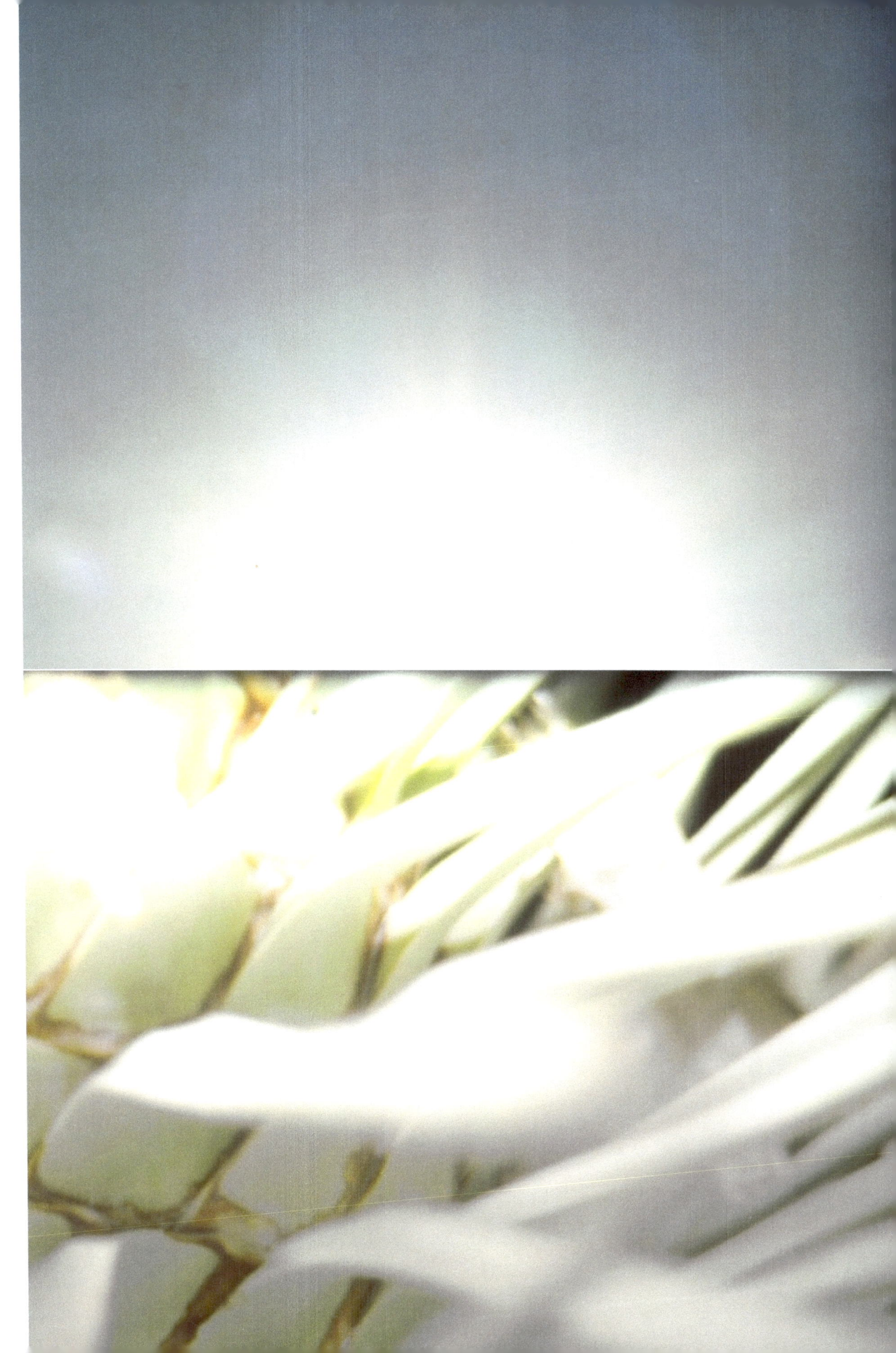

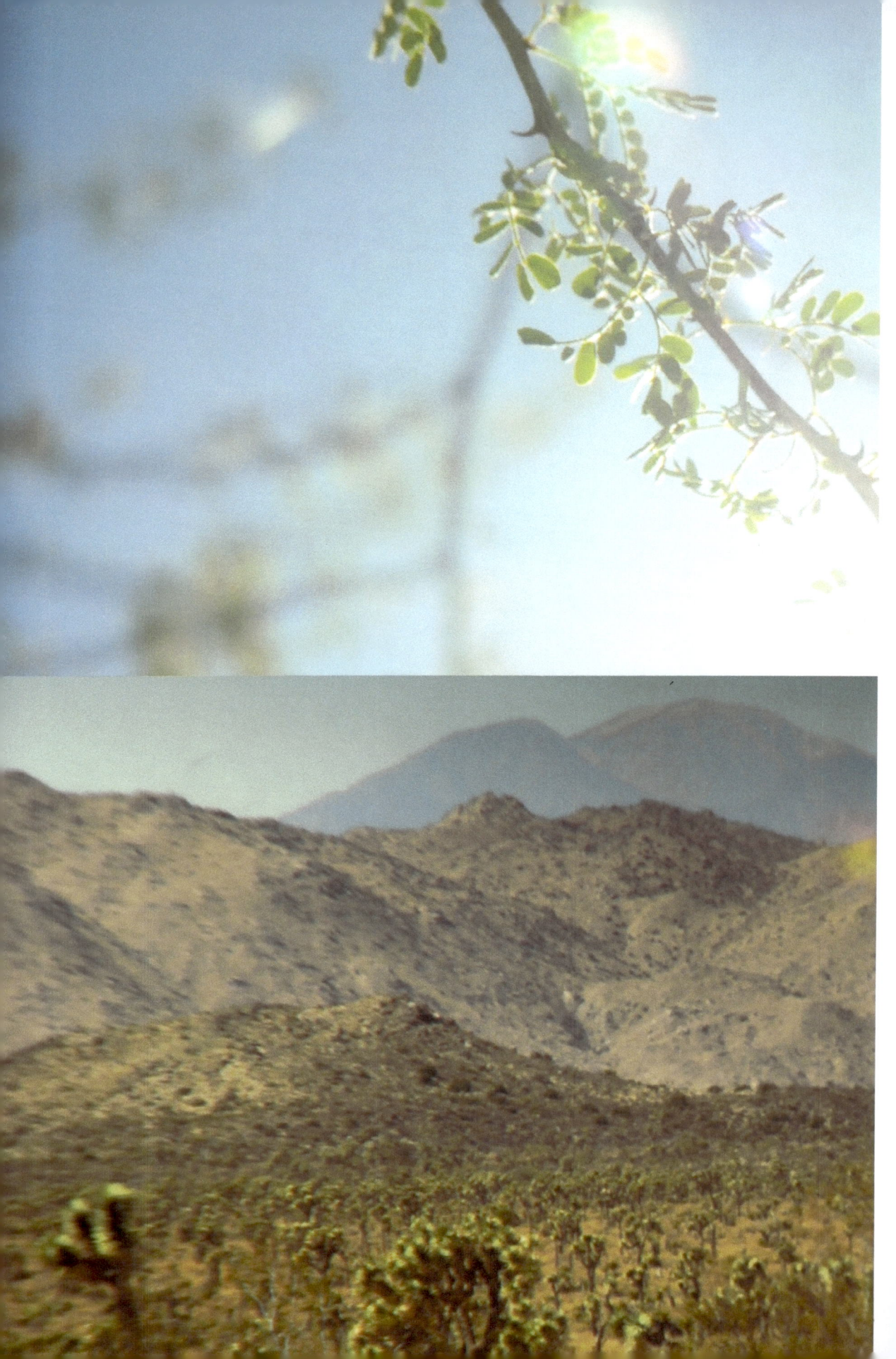

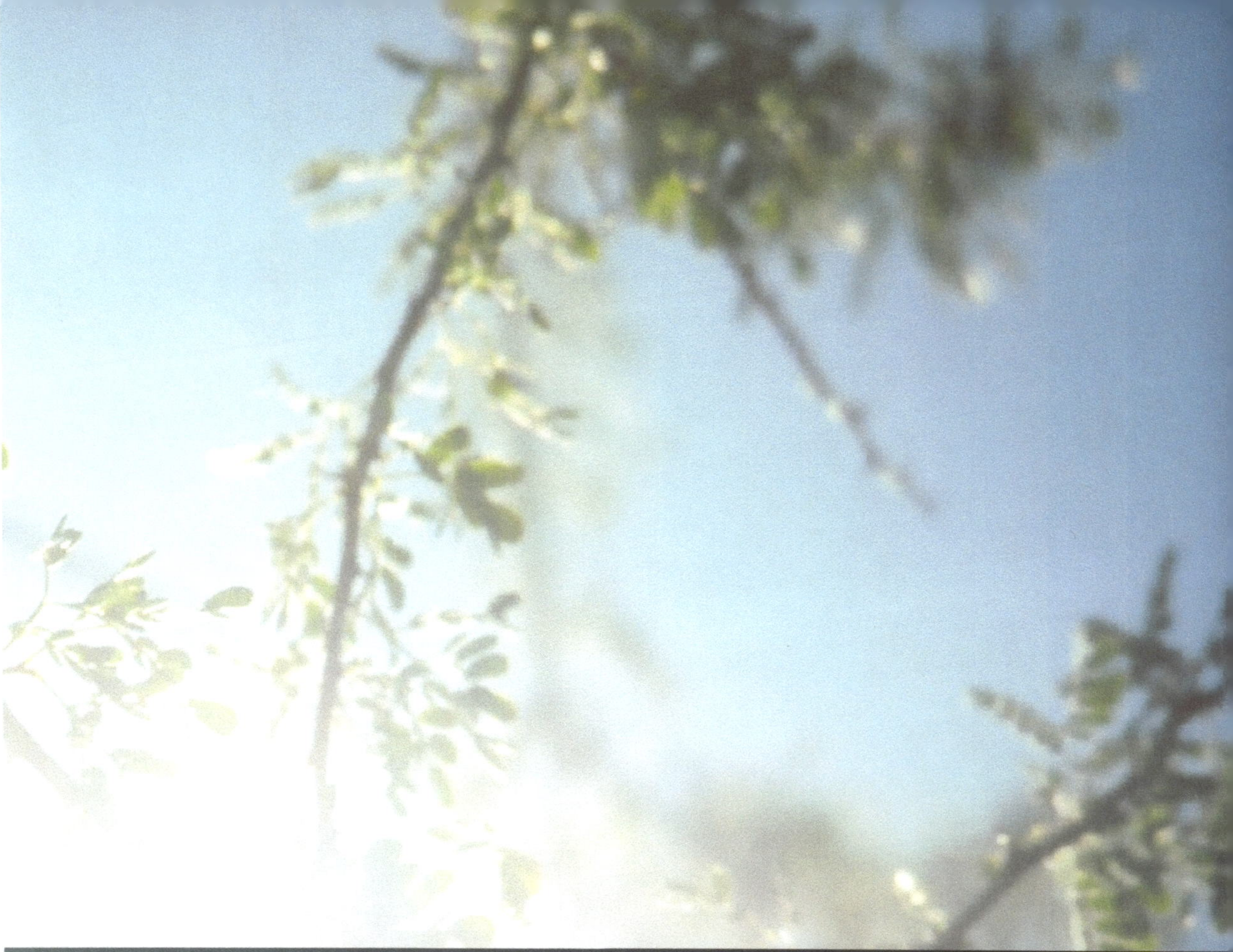
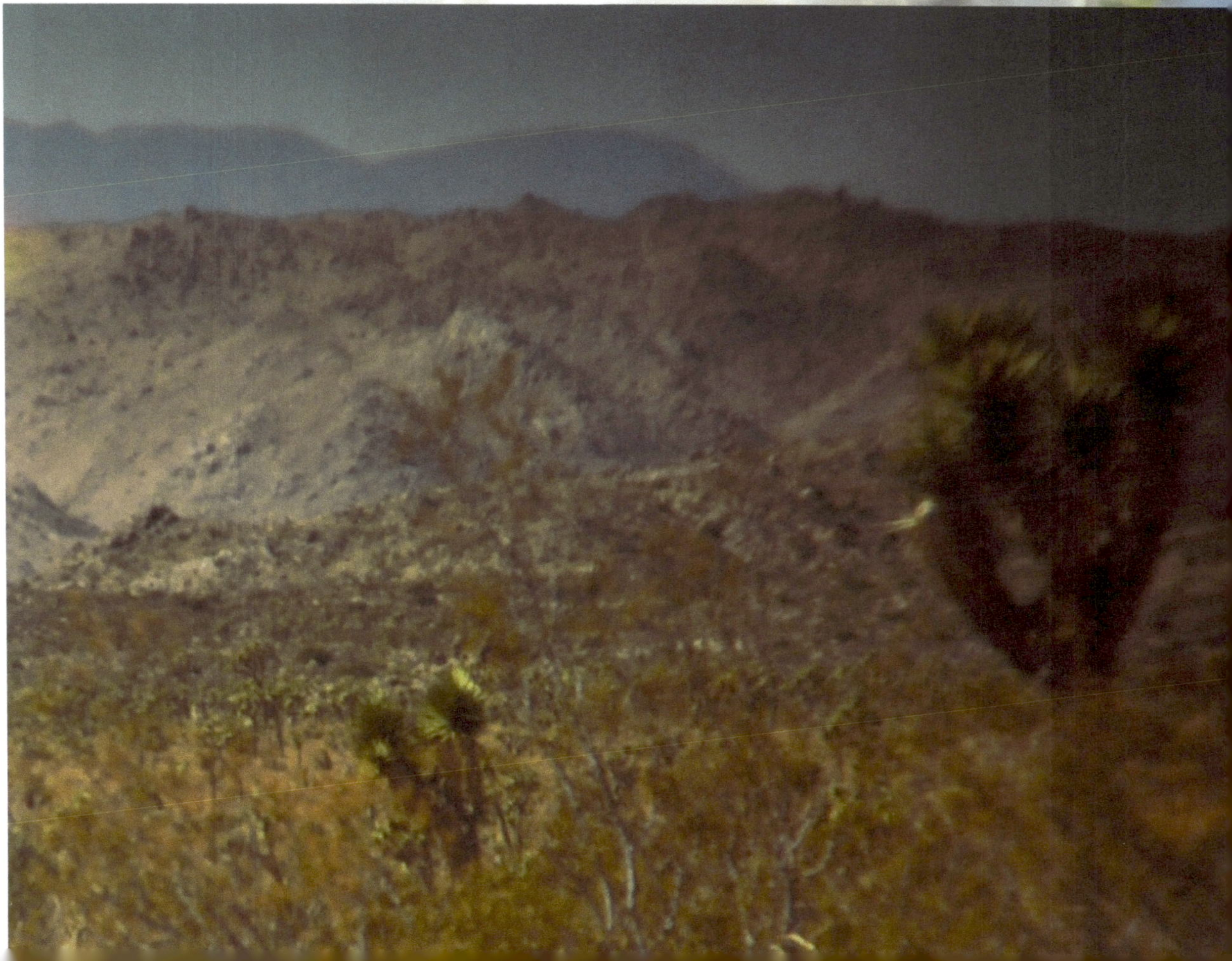

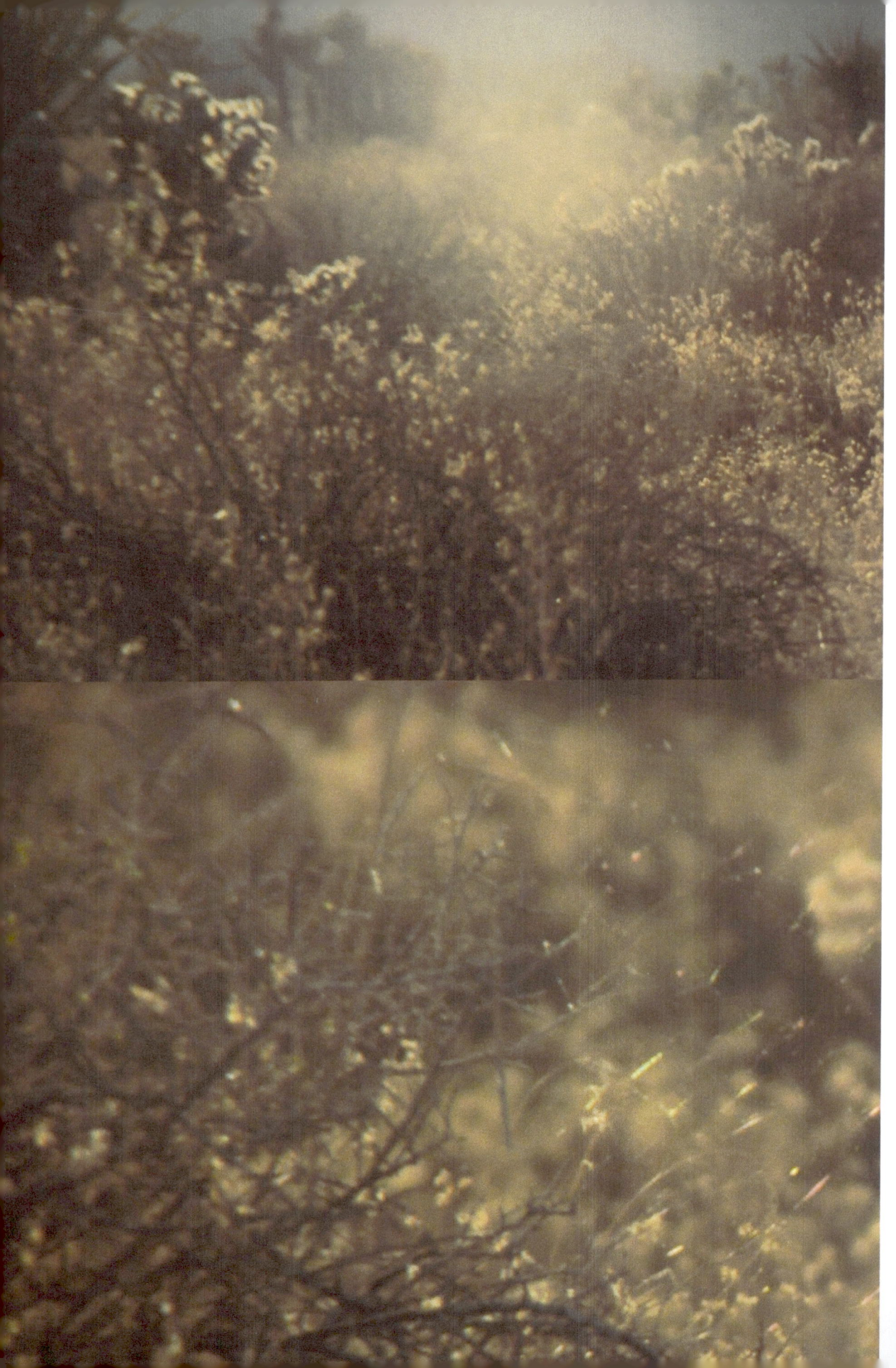

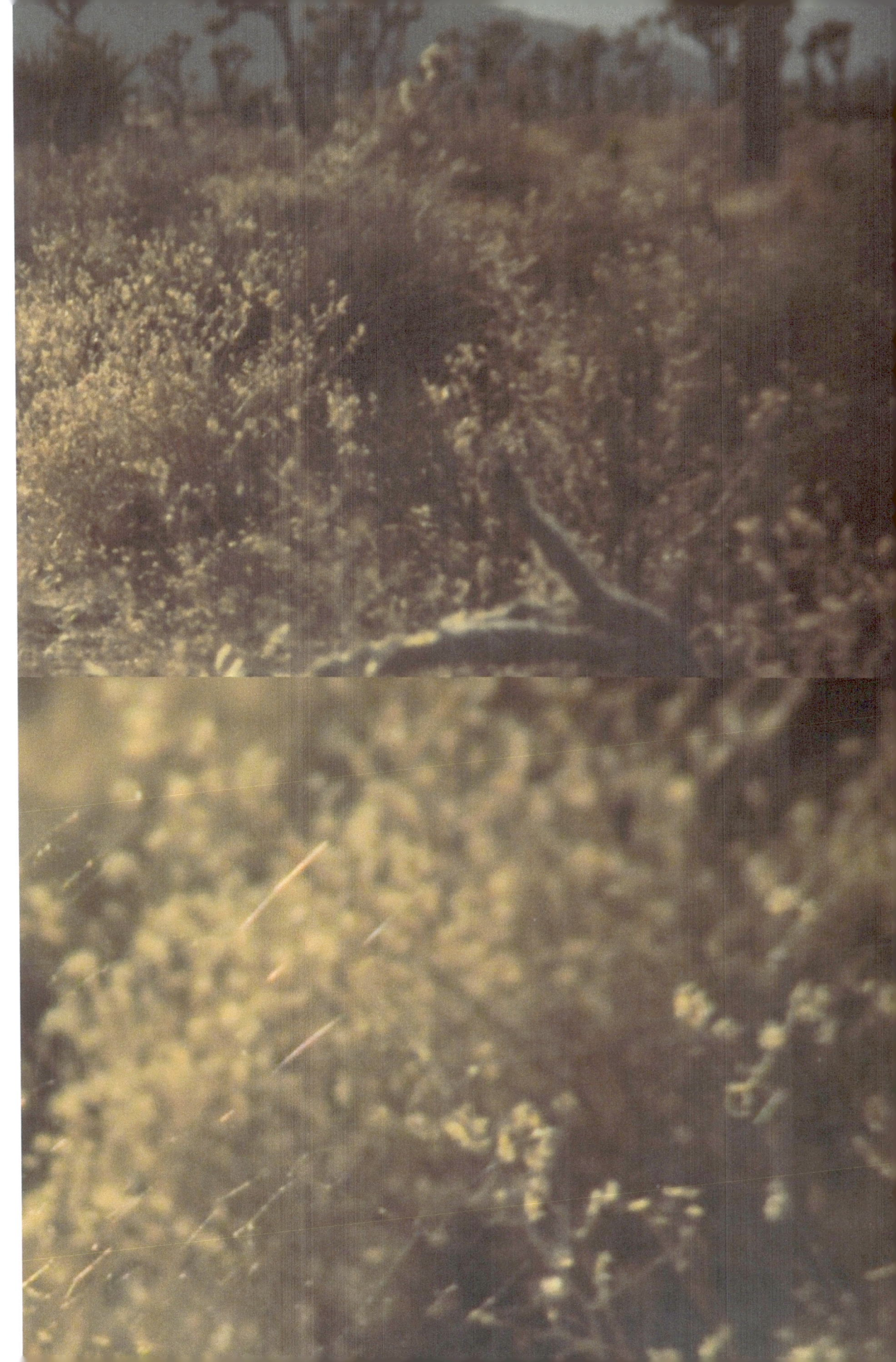

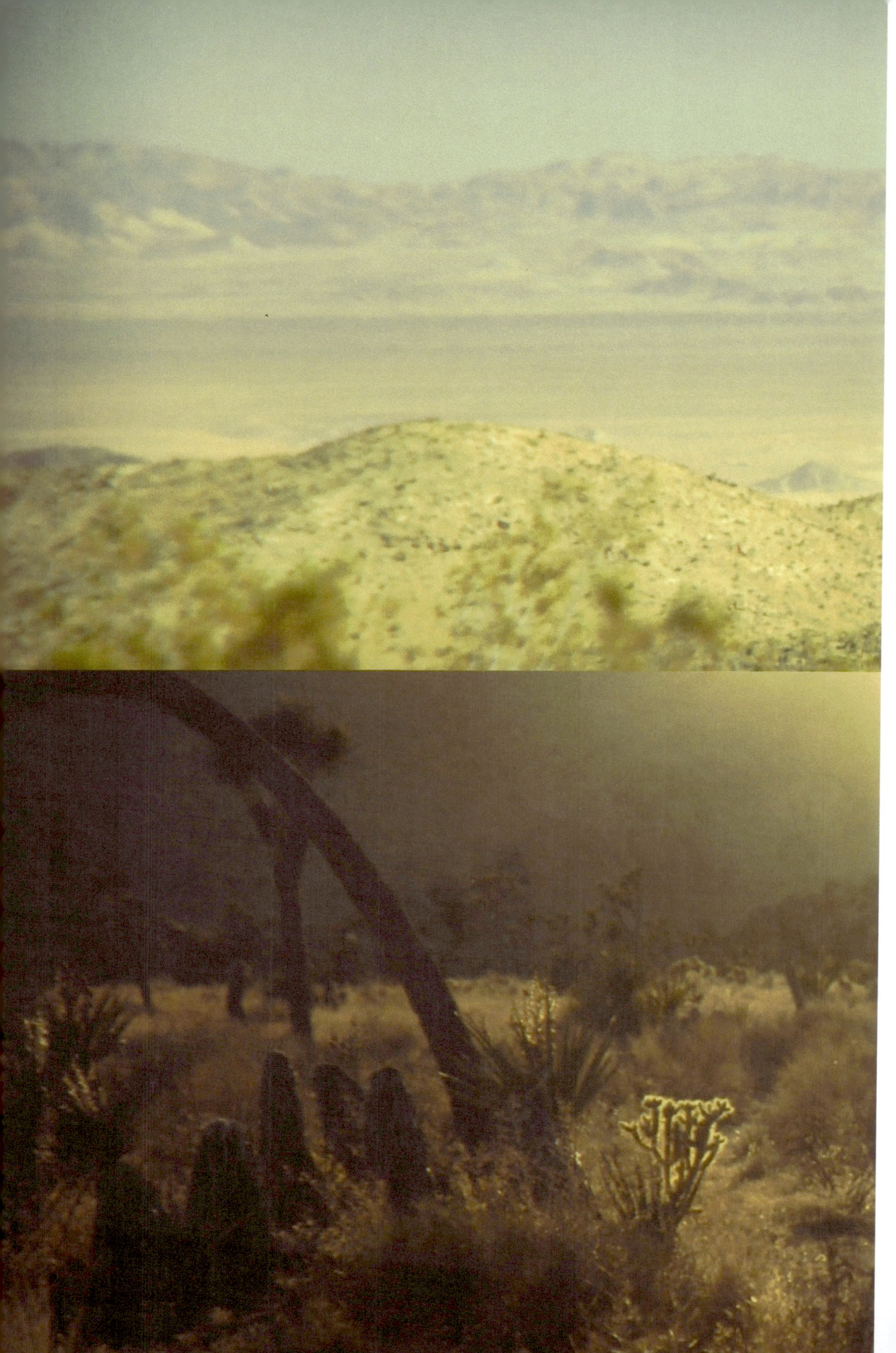

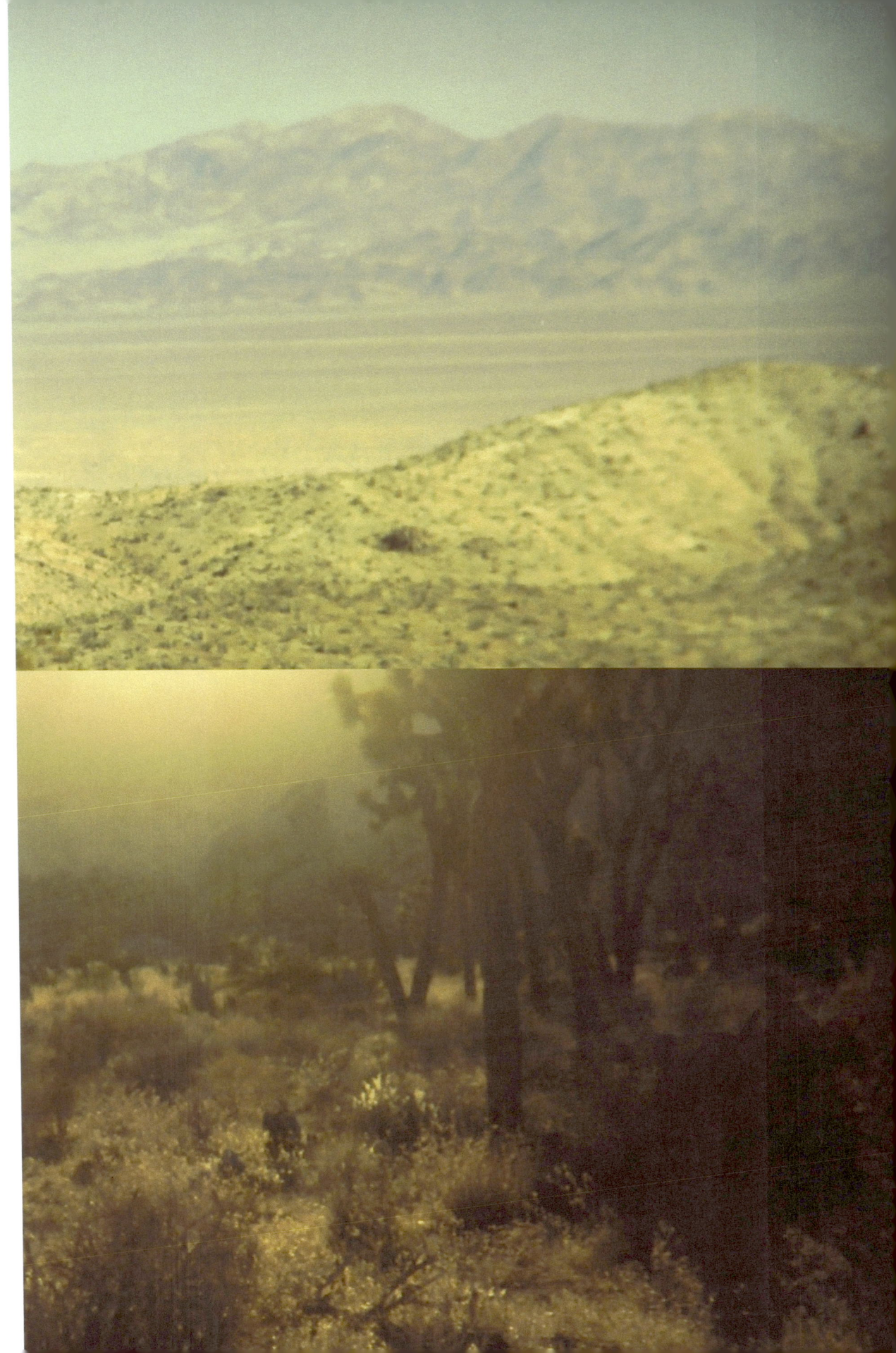

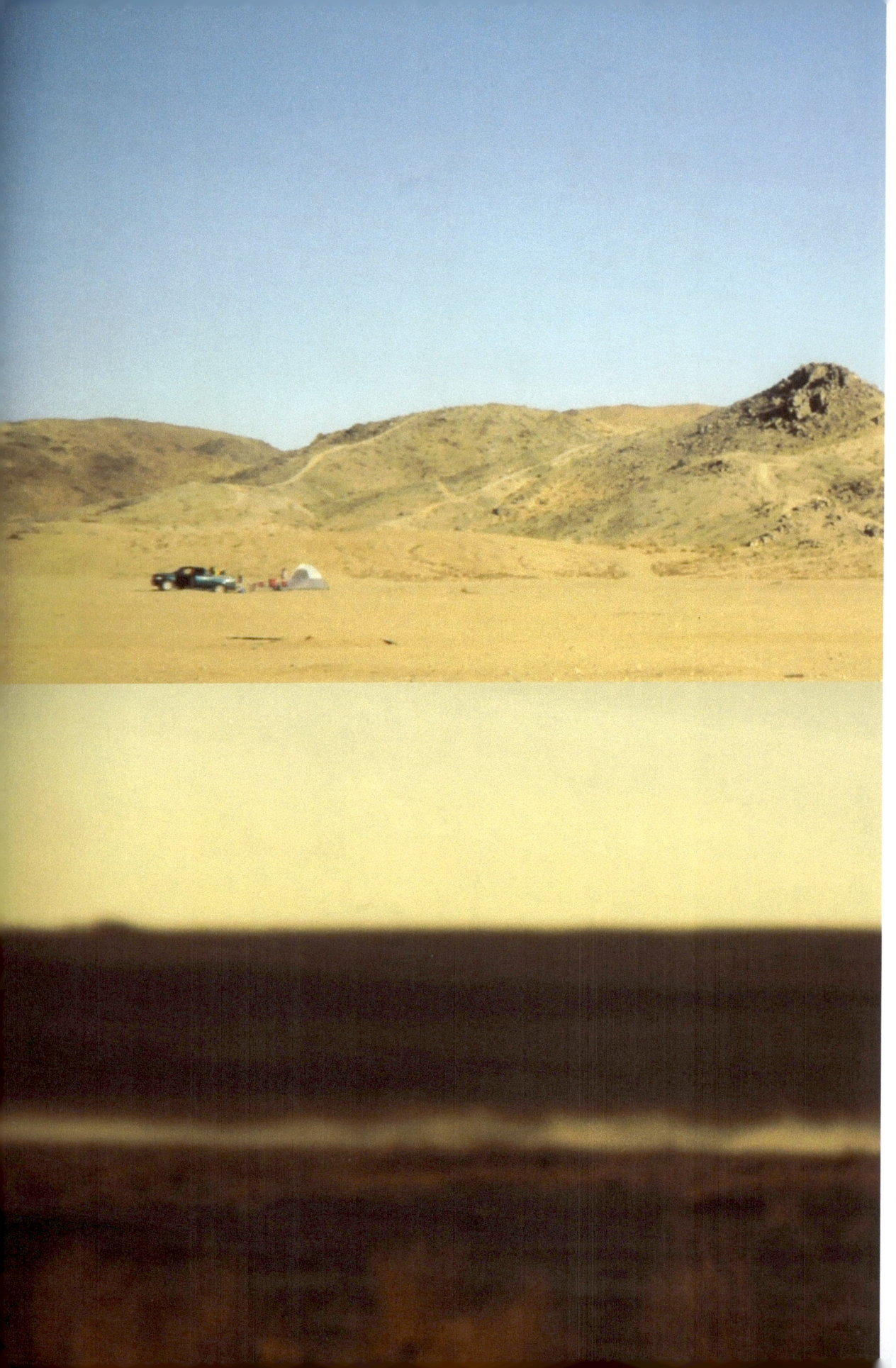

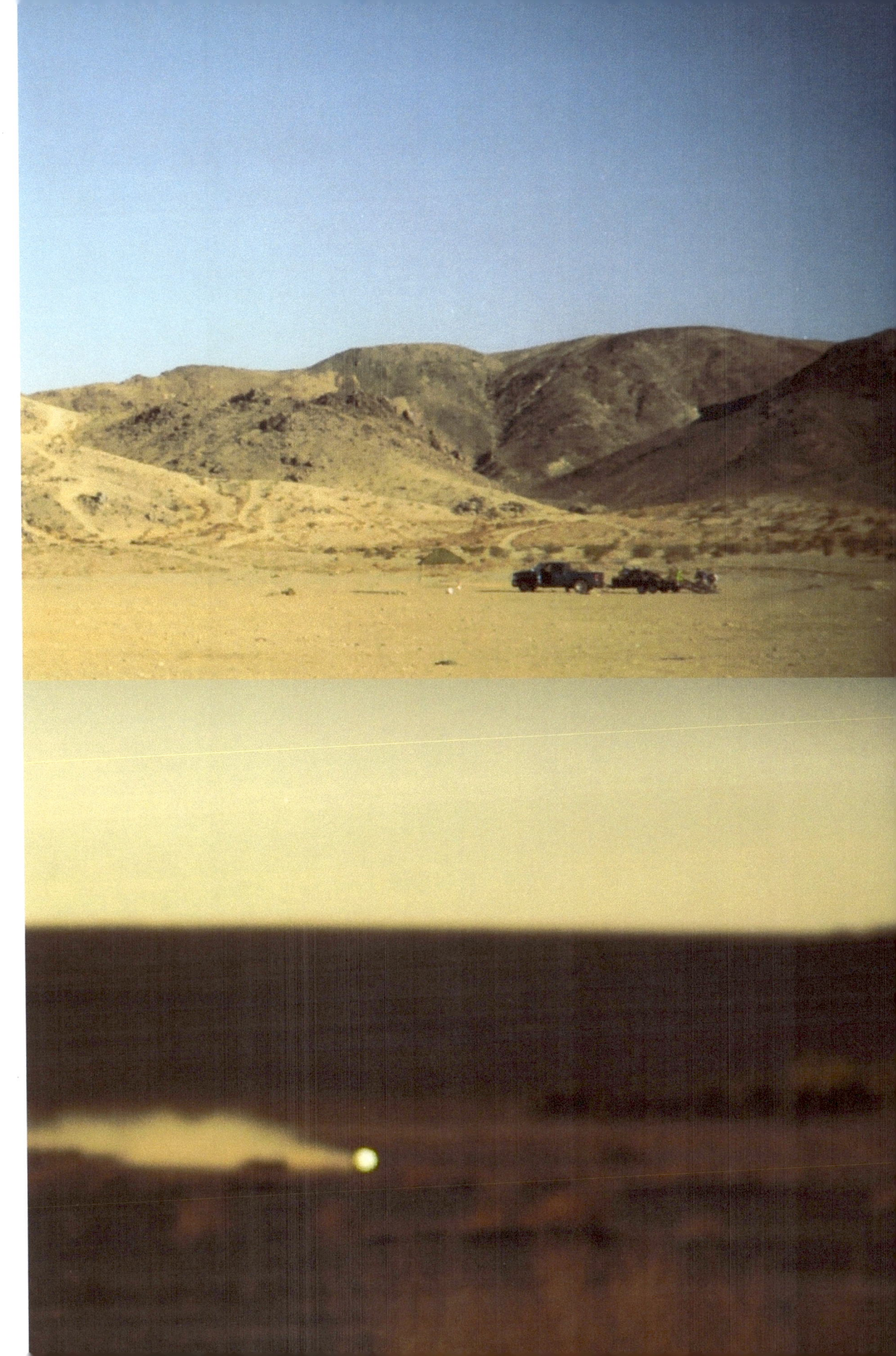

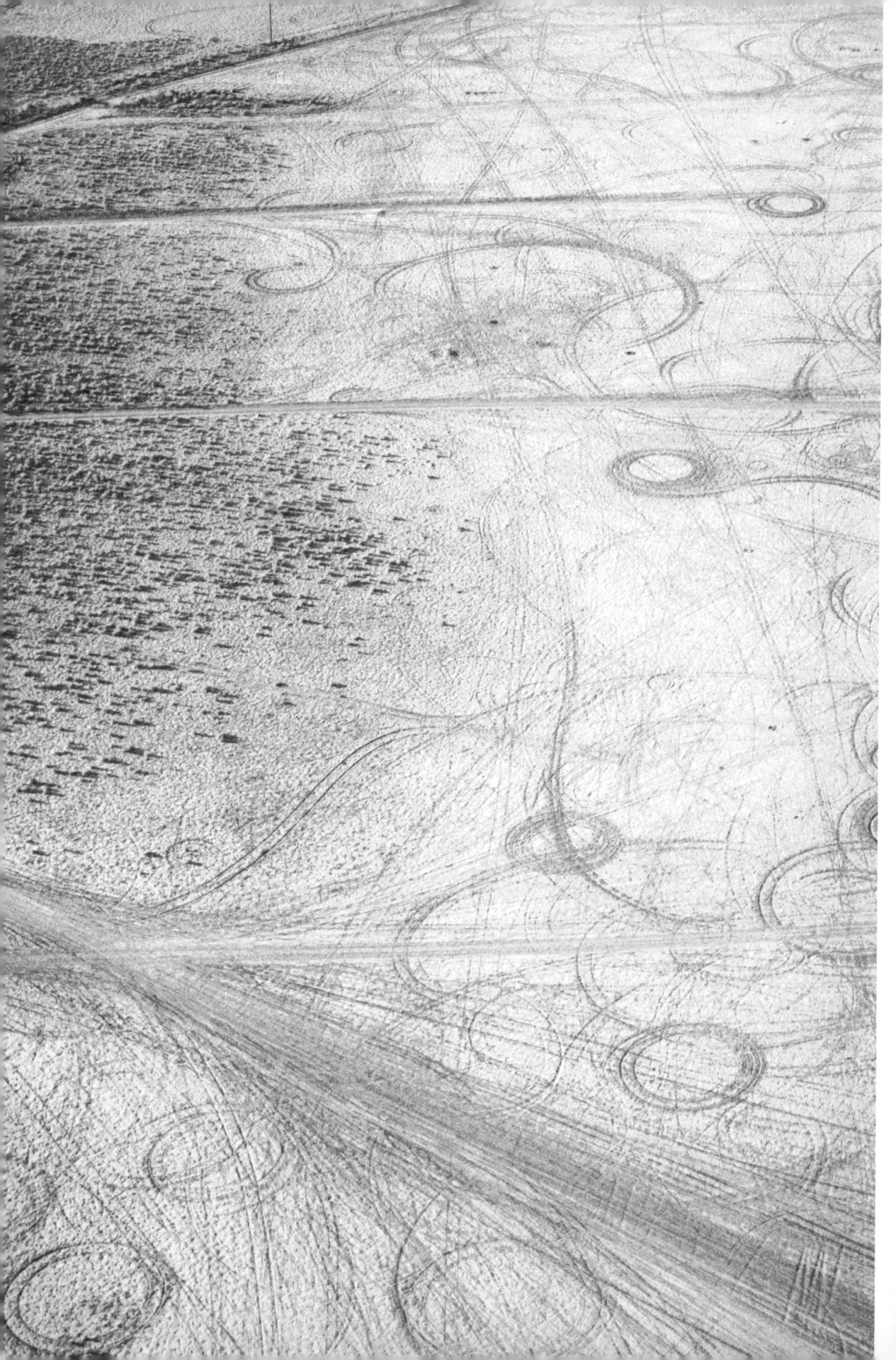

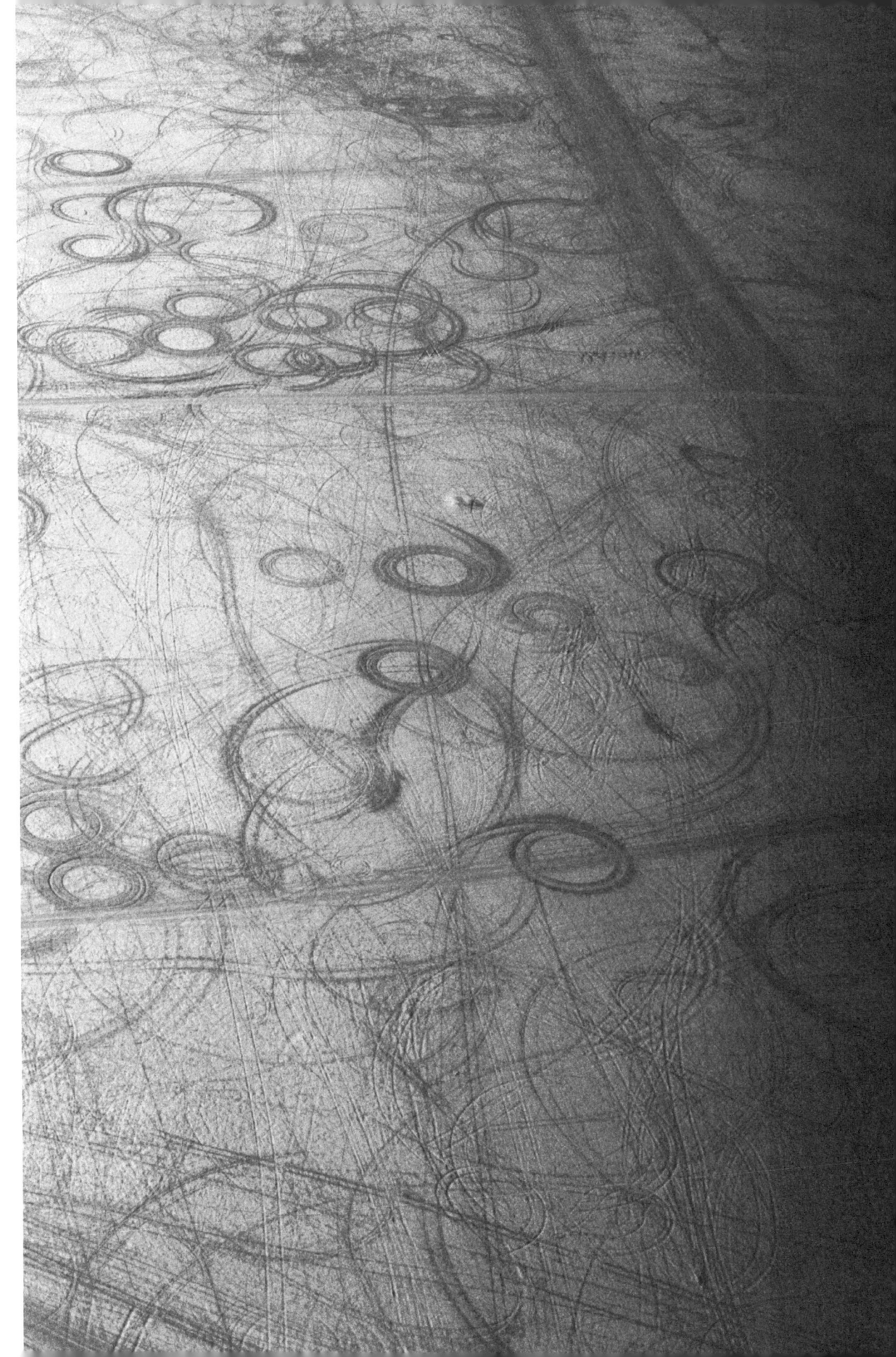

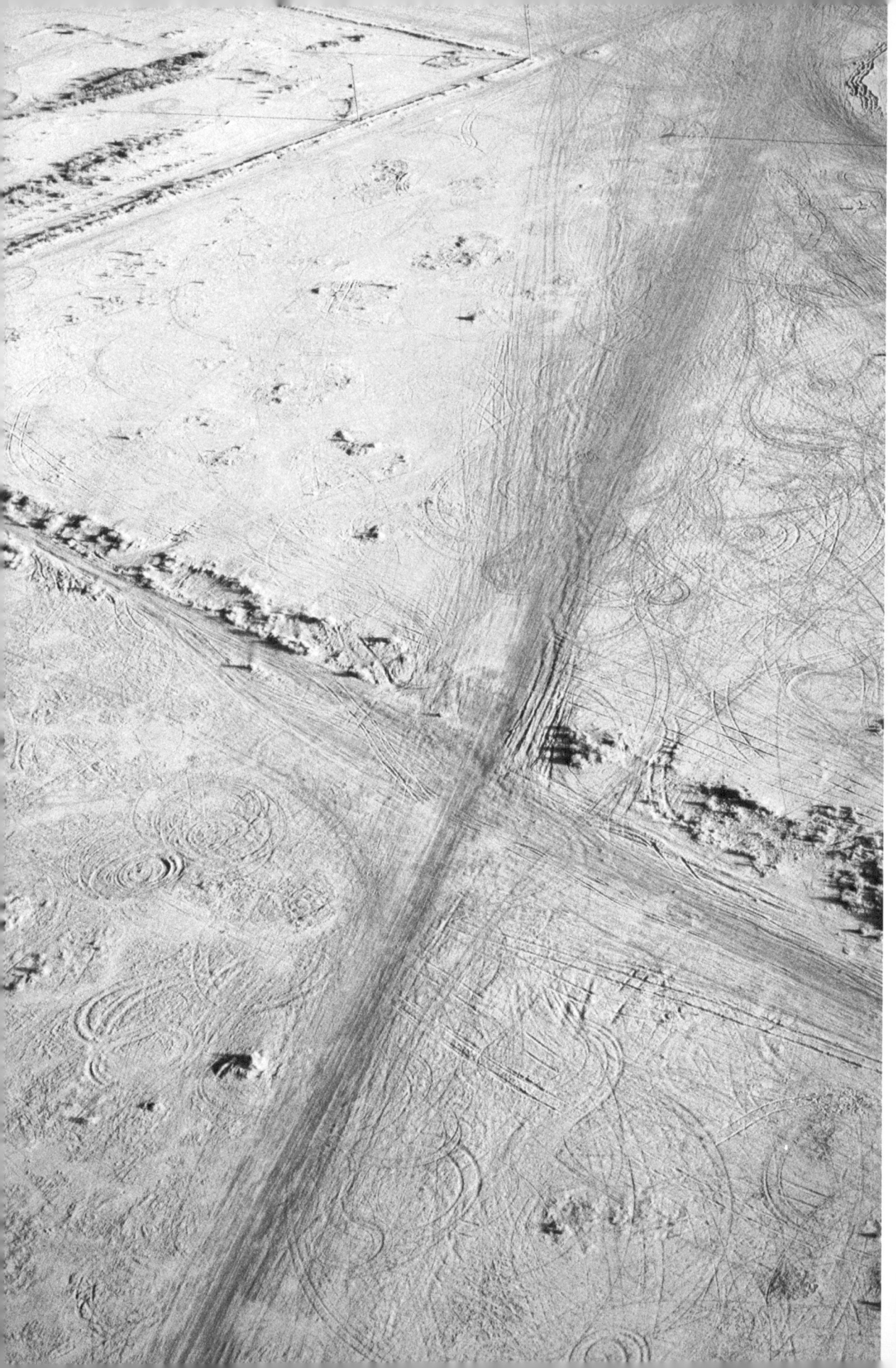

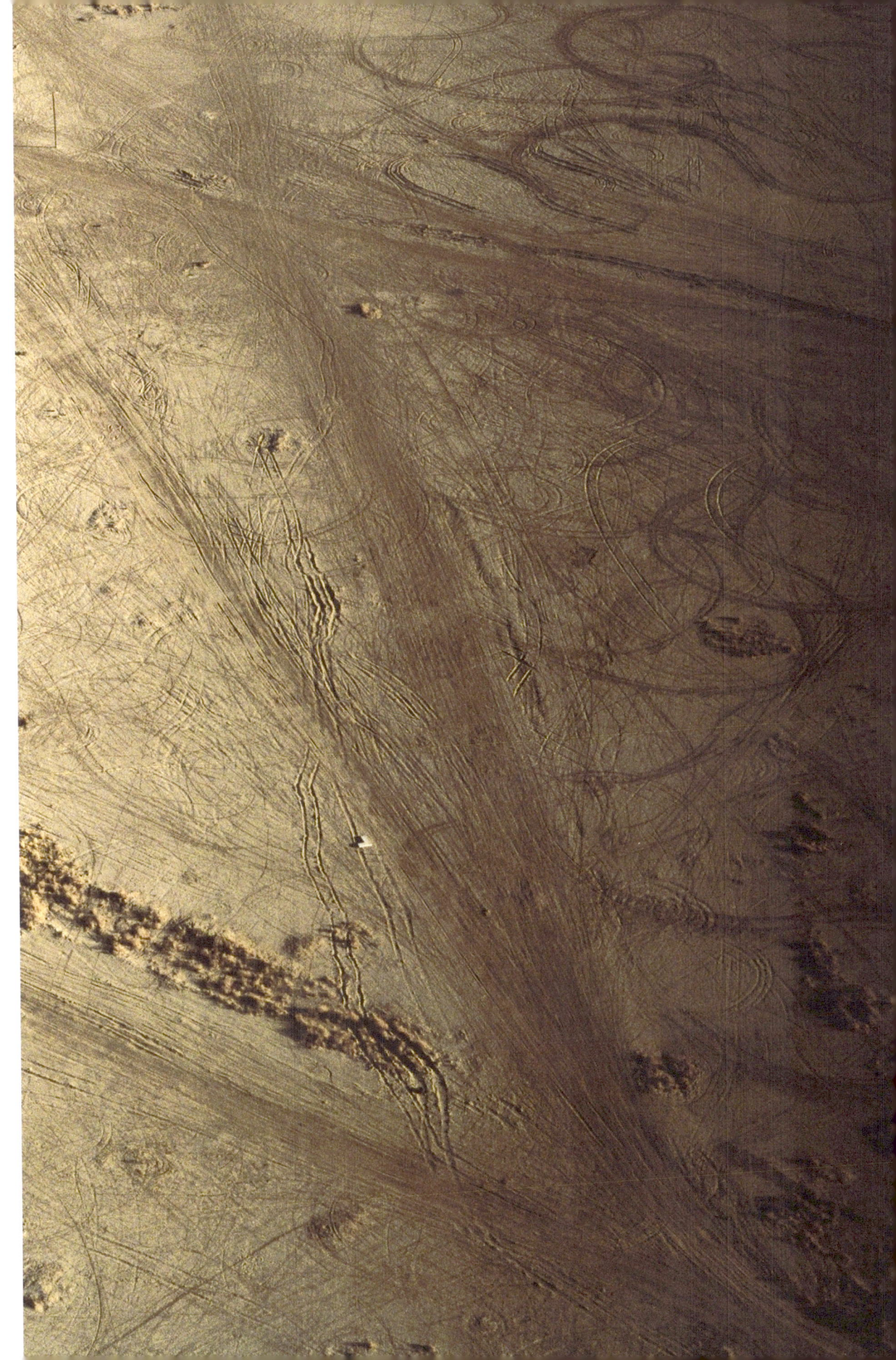

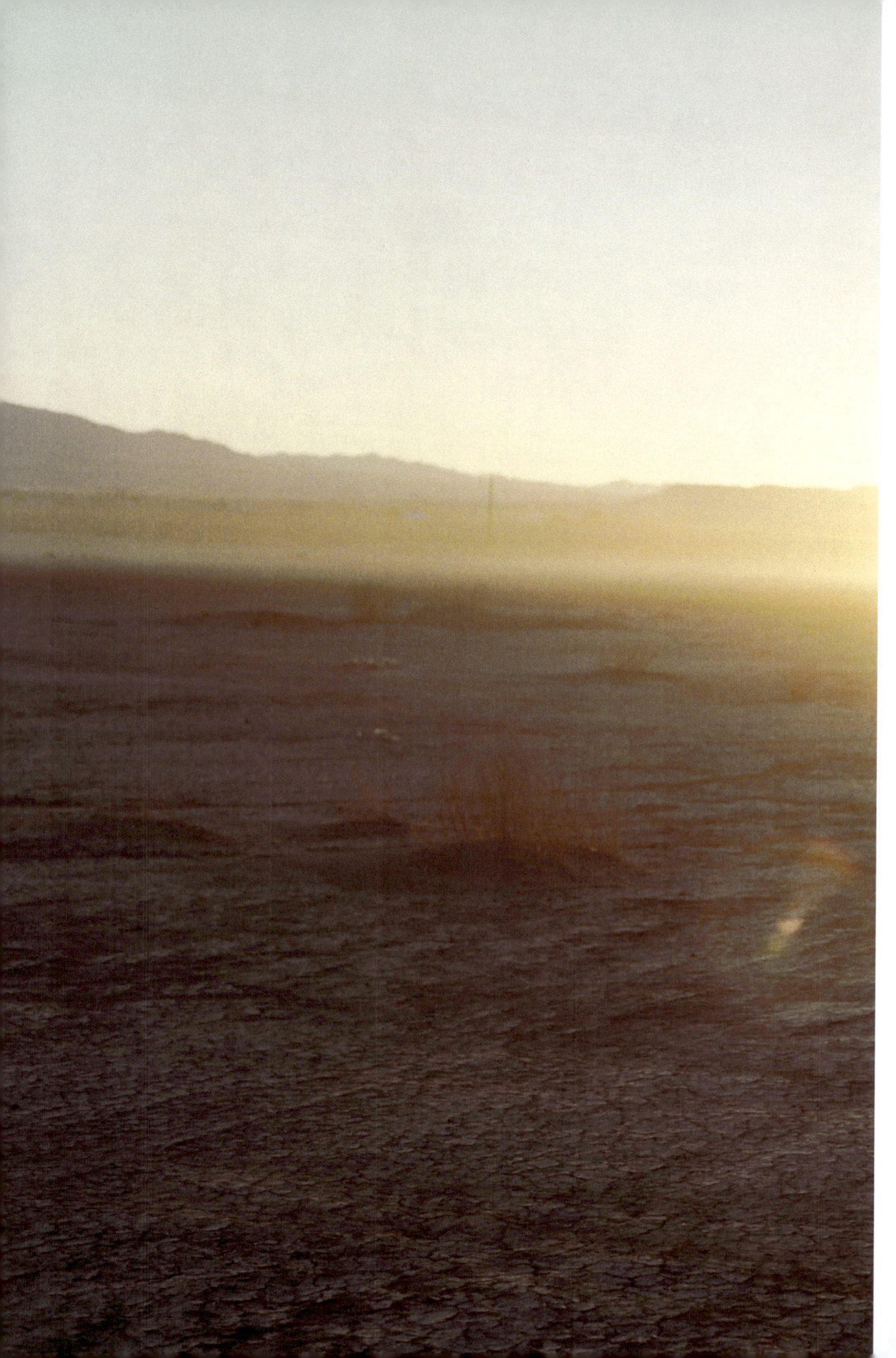

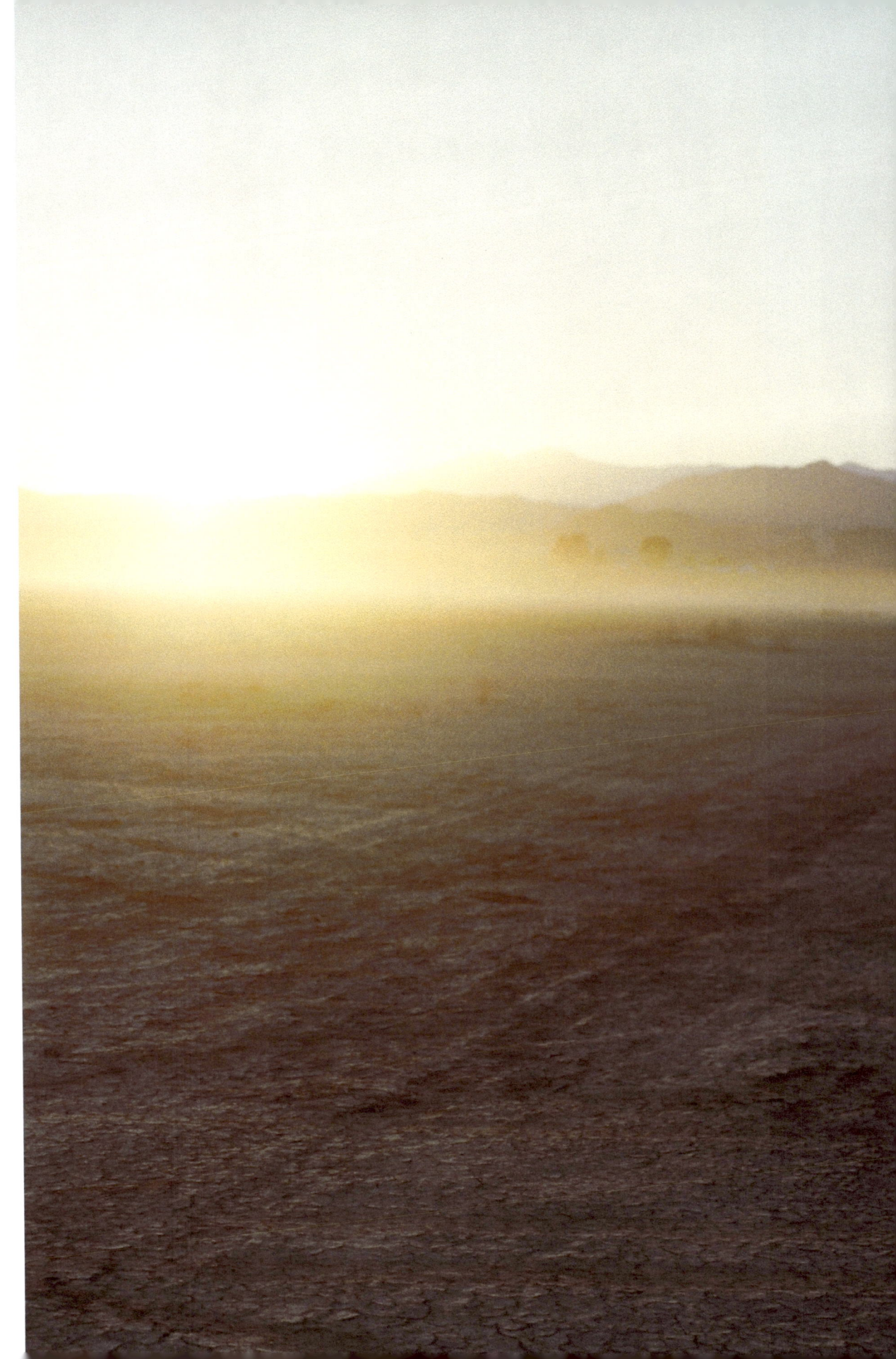

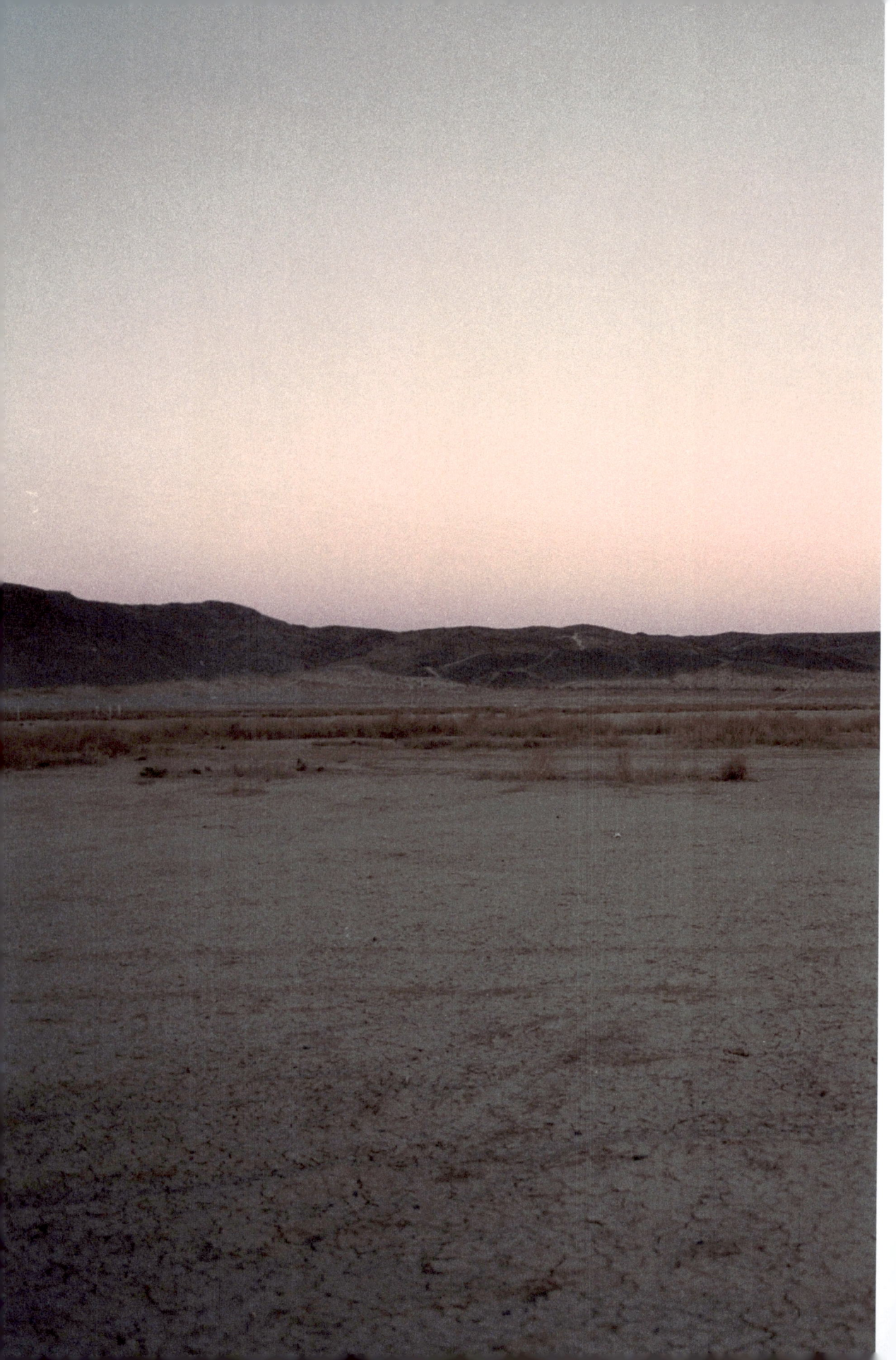

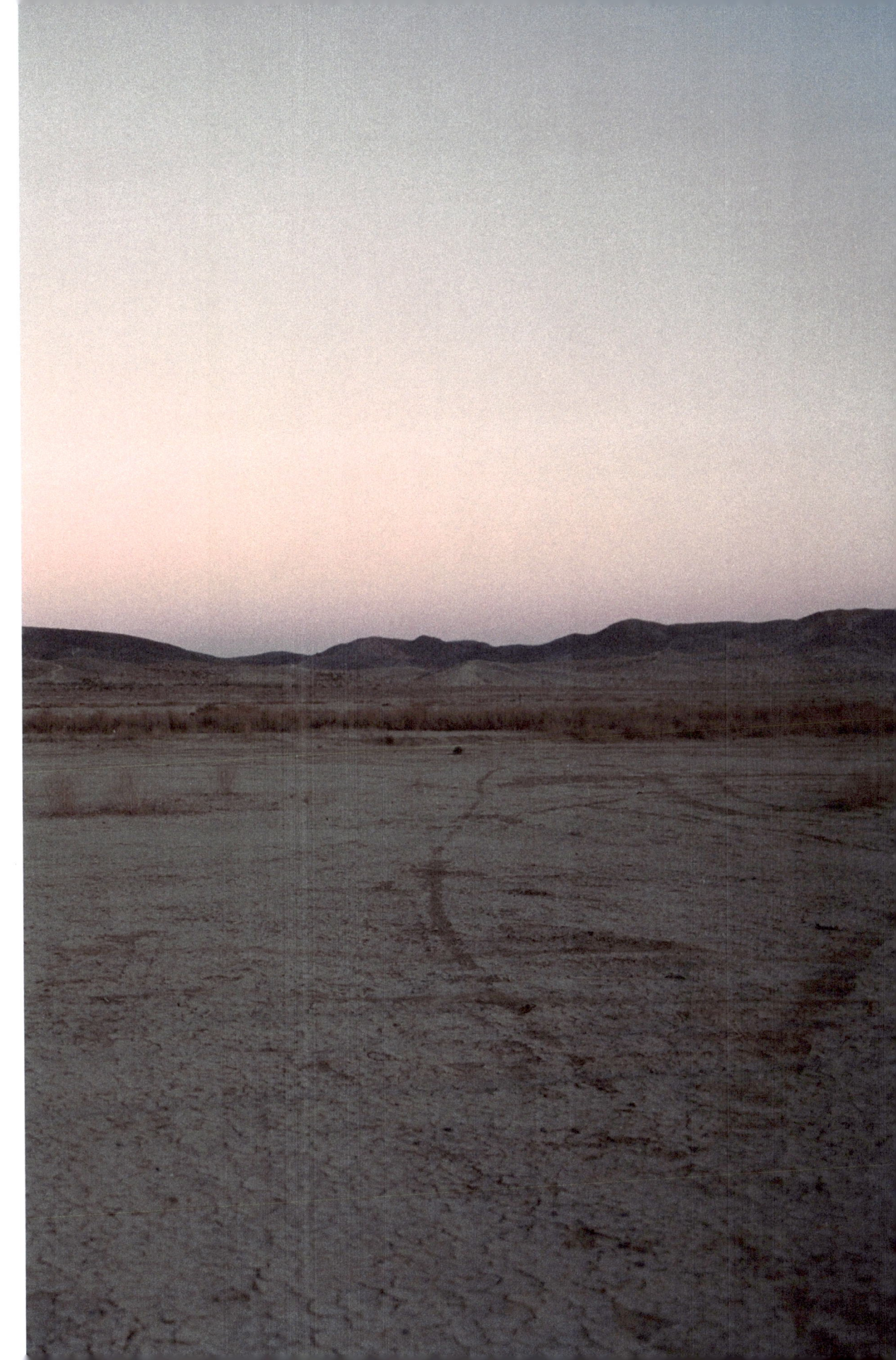

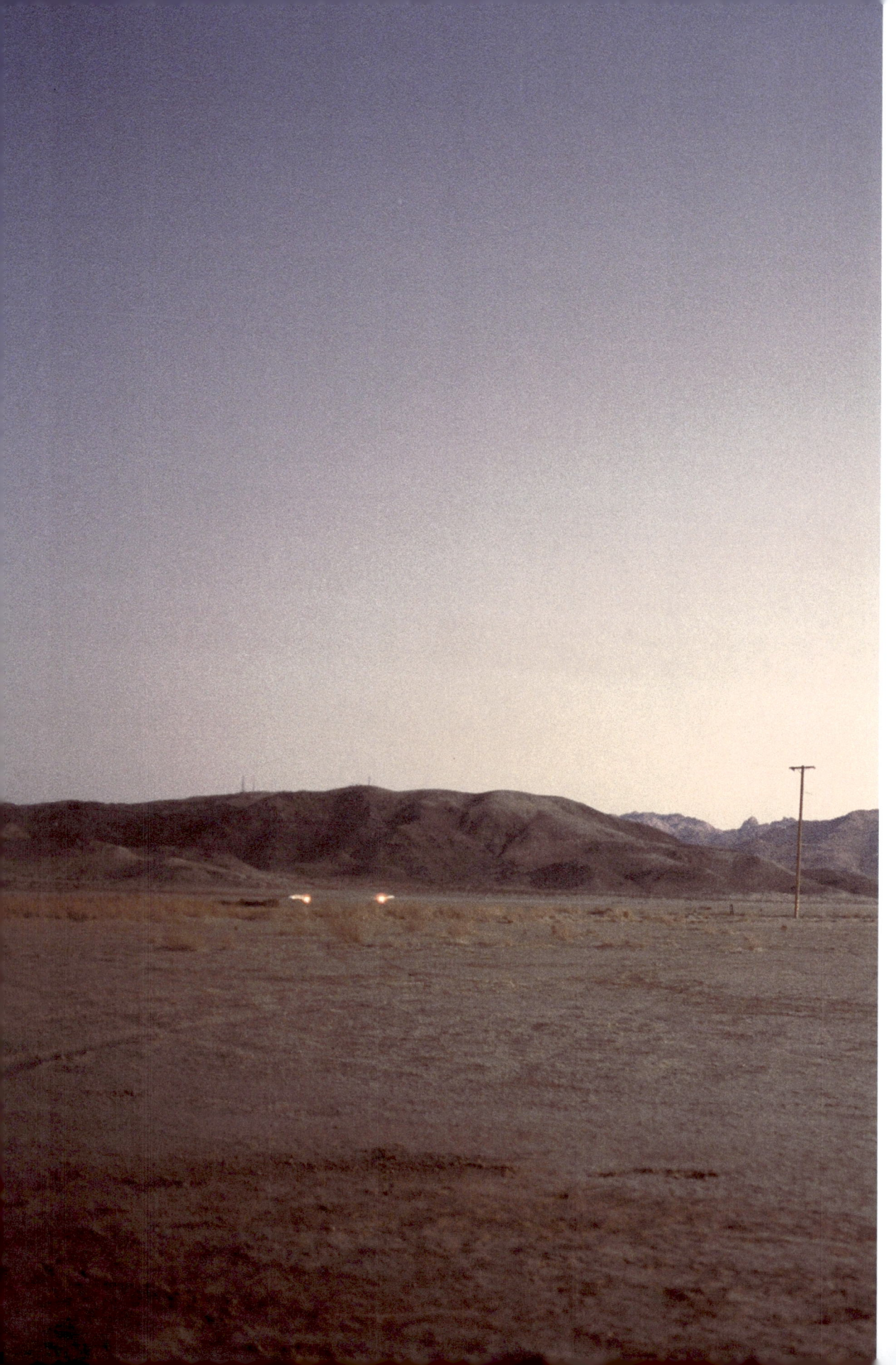

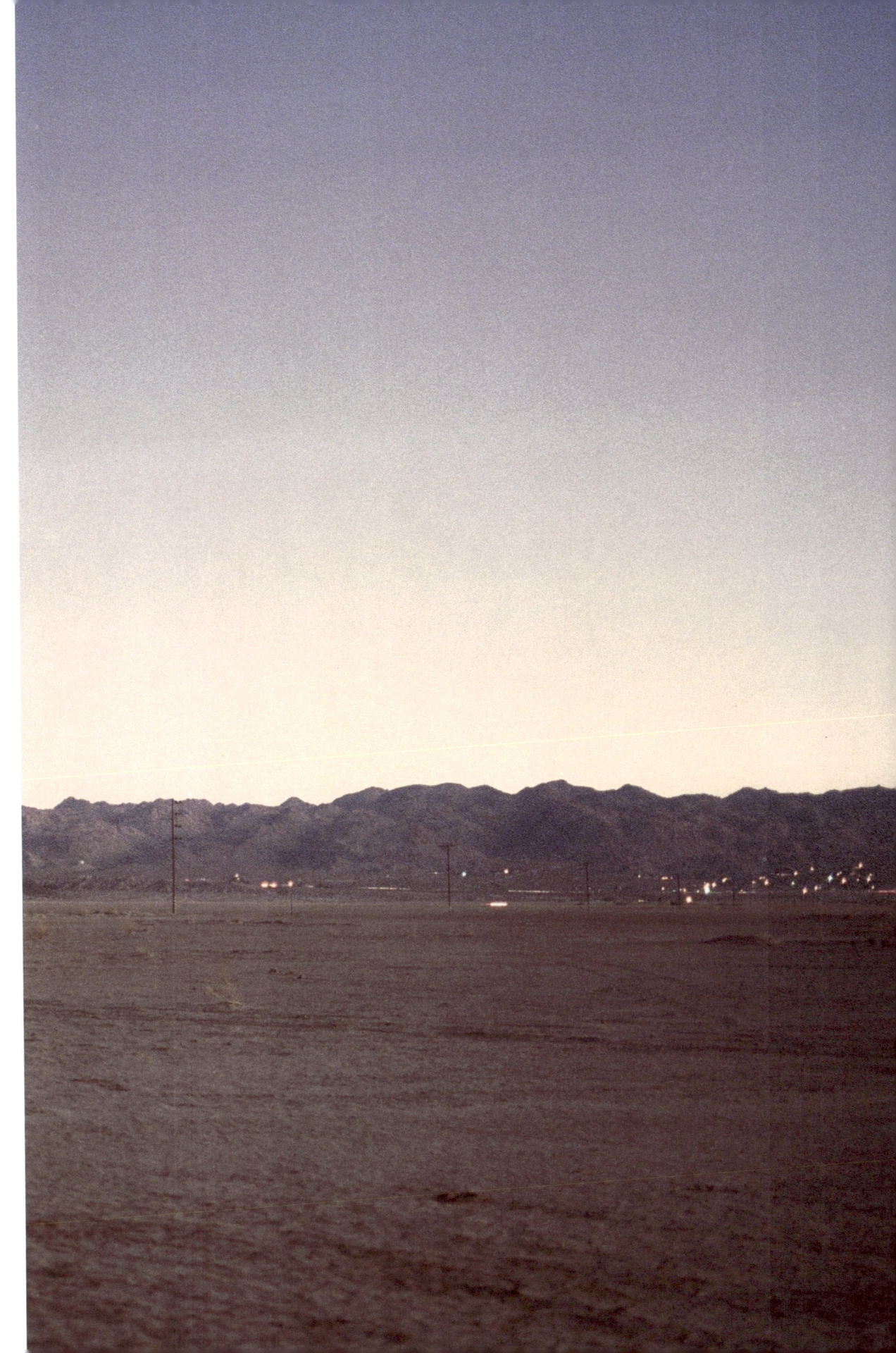

Amanda Law: How long were you on location working on *Desert* (2010)? Was there a period of immersion before you began working on the piece, or how was your time structured?

Jesse Fleming: For one month I lived twenty miles into Joshua Tree National Park. I stayed in a cabin down a dirt road, off the grid, with no means of communication. Water was tanked in and power was limited to solar and battery. I put together the shoot when I got there. The idea was immersion and reaction – a documentation of myself in the desert and the record of that time. I would wake up at sunrise and begin filming. The daily practice was based around a car, a camera pack, and a map. I would pick an area or direction and if it had an interesting feeling to it, hike from there. Time was spent drifting, shooting, studying, and building on each preceding day.

AL: How do you think the length of your immersion played a role in your observations of the desert?

JF: The month gave me enough time to get a feeling for everything. Sometimes I got a little kooky, sometimes it was total silence and serenity. It was enough to get a read on a very resonant and alien landscape.

AL: What was your understanding of the desert before and after your time there?

JF: I had thought of the desert as a dead space, but then I took a trip to the Sahara in Northern Africa. I was floored by the sand dunes; they continued into the horizon in all directions. It was a slow-moving and evolving sea blown by wind, alive and in flux, but under different terms than I was used to. There was a prevailing silence that was ironically loud and hypnotic. The guide told me, "The secret is in the silence." That stuck with me. It left me wanting to find out what that meant. Joshua Tree was a follow up to that.

AL: What are your observations of Joshua Tree versus other deserts?

JF: There is a language that varies among deserts; vibration may be a better term. The Sahara was oceanic: mostly calm, expansive, and terrible without proper supplies. Joshua Tree was alien, like life on Mars, maybe. It has an odd and sometimes discomforting murmur at night. I remember thinking it was like an ancient grandfather figure that has a lot to teach you, but would also like to eat you.

AL: What was your editing process like?

JF: It took me about a year before I was ready to start editing. I didn't know how to work with the footage. Originally I wanted the project to be landscape only, but then some friends came to visit me in Joshua Tree and we wound up going to an off-road vehicle area. I became curious about the patterns made by the vehicle tracks and hired an airplane to shoot some aerial footage. The tracks looked like something in between land art and crop circles. I decided to build the project around the idea of the landscape, the language of the landscape, and its' subconscious effects on the people who inhabited it. When I went out for a return visit a year later I showed a JTNP botanist an aerial photograph and she said "Oh man, that looks just like particle collision". Later she sent me an image from The Fermi National Accelerator Laboratory. Side by side, the aerial photograph and the microscopic image are oddly similar. I didn't assume this to be evidence, but it was interesting because particle collision deals with cosmology and the origins of life. I appreciated the coincidence and it got me going. I started editing with this in mind and after a few weeks I felt like the piece started to show itself.

AL: The edits in *Desert* are often abrupt and harsh. Can you explain what role the cuts play?

JF: I wanted to work with varying time expectancy. In a durational piece, the longer you're forced to sit in front of a work, the more your perception starts to warp in and out of the ordinary time expectancy. Some of the landscape shots are static compositions that hold for a while. When the timing lingers our observations wander and we start to notice all of the little details and the expanded life of the scene. In contrast, I used abrupt and harsh edits as a mode to drive, offset, disturb, or shift the viewer's perception.

AL: *Desert* seems to have been influenced by artists such as Michael Heizer, Robert Irwin, and Robert Smithson. How does your work differ from the work of these artists?

JF: I went into the desert and recorded my response to things as they were, or as I perceived them. Then I edited the material to complete the project. When Heizer and Smithson worked in the desert, they altered the landscape and documented the action or completion of that process. In Irwin's case he decided not to work directly with the desert but to reconstruct the essence of his experiences in an outside context.

AL: Why did you decide to do a photo book?

JF: I had a series of photographs taken at Joshua Tree that I wanted to work with, but in the same way that I had trouble knowing what to do with the video footage, I had difficulty knowing how to work with the photographs as single images. The book legitimatized the single image and expanded the concepts of the project by using images and contexts not included in the video.

AL: How does the project operate in the book versus the video?

JF: The goal between the book and the video are the same. They point at our relationship to landscape outside of natural science and into the realm of phenomenology. The difference between the two is how the viewer experiences the project in time. The video is looped whereas the viewer determines the pacing of the book.

AL: How did you determine the sequence of the images in the book?

JF: In the beginning, I had the photos arranged as an essay. Over time I realized that structured this way they functioned as individual images. When I started focusing more on the sequencing than the single image, and including the abstract imagery from the video *It*, the book started working for me. It allowed me to create a non-linear narrative oscillating between the abstract and the literal.

AL: I noticed that you brought another video piece into the book, *It* (2010). What was the idea behind that inclusion?

JF: *It* was a work that came after *Desert*, and was in part, born from it. *It* had given me the ability to work with other ideas I had been playing with on non-language and sensorial work. I wanted to make something that would shut down our analytical system. I felt like *Desert* informed *It* and *It* made *Desert* more complete. Where *Desert* functions as a hypnotic fever dream *It* was a distillation of the elements - light, atmospheric perspective, sound, shape, and color.

AL: Being a wholly abstract piece, I find *It* more difficult to discuss since there are no real-world references. Did you have a mystical or spiritual experience that led to your inspiration?

JF: I went to the desert to understand "the secret in the silence" but found it unintelligible. So I drew connections to the parts of the place that seemed related such as the people, the evidence of people, and the patterns or cycles of the place. In this way I could map the "silence" without knowing what it was. It occurred to me that "the secret in the silence" could be interpreted as letting go of the desire to understand in order to arrive closer to it.

Amanda Law is an experimental and documentary filmmaker in Los Angeles. She works at the Hammer Museum as New Media Associate.

THANK YOU

Jim Bagley
Lawrence Barth
Dylan Chandler
Mike Cipra
Jane Cipra
Caron Davidson
Cindy Dean
Anat Ebgi
Jean Fleming
Randall Fleming
Daniel Foster
Brock Hammond
George Hass
Danny Kelley
Brandon Klein
Amanda Law
Davon Ramos
Jody Rassel
Chris Reding
Royce Robertson
Chris Seguine
Peter Strietmann
Starr Sutherland
Gretchen Vater
Jeffery Wells

www.ingramcontent.com/pod-product-compliance
Lightning Source LLC
Chambersburg PA
CBHW050747180526
45159CB00003B/1380